Also by Neale S. Godfrey:

Money Doesn't Grow on Trees
Why Money Was Invented
Here's the Scoop: Follow an Ice Cream Cone Around the World
Follow a Dollar Around Town

A Penny Saved

Teaching Your Children the Values and Life Skills They Will Need to Live in the Real World

Neale S. Godfrey
with Tad Richards

A Fireside Book
Published by Simon & Schuster
New York   London   Toronto   Sydney   Tokyo   Singapore

FIRESIDE
Rockefeller Center
1230 Avenue of the Americas
New York, NY 10020

First Fireside Edition 1996

FIRESIDE and colophon are registered trademarks
of Simon & Schuster Inc.

Designed by Bonni Leon-Berman

Manufactured in the United States of America

1 3 5 7 9 10 8 6 4 2

Library of Congress Cataloging-in-Publication Data
Godfrey, Neale S.
A penny saved : teaching your children the values and life skills they
will need to live in the real world / Neale Godfrey with Tad Richards
p.   cm.
Includes index.
1. Children—Finance, Personal.   2. Teenagers—Finance, Personal.
3. Children's allowances.   4. Saving and thrift.   I. Richards, Tad.
II. Title.
HG179.G633   1995
332.024—dc20   95-12111 CIP

ISBN 0-684-80397-6
0-684-82480-9 (Pbk)

Dedication

This book is dedicated to my pride and joy.

Pride when Oprah Winfrey asked him, "I don't get it—you mean if you don't do every single job, you don't get paid anything at all?" and he looked up at her, unhesitating, and said, "No work, no pay. That's the way it works."

Pride when she passed up the chance to go on Oprah's show because her school forensics team needed her for their statewide meet, and she'd made the commitment to them (she won second place in New Jersey).

Pride when he gave his allowance to a homeless woman to buy food and told well-meaning adults who questioned him: "You help people out when they need it. I work hard for my money, and I have a right to do what I want with it. And I want to share it."

Pride when she heard about a local family who had lost their home to a fire, and she took it upon herself to organize a relief effort at her school and in the community, providing clothing and support for the family.

Pride for their generosity, their charitable work, their deeply in-grained sense of responsibility in maintaining their longterm savings.

Joy in their humor and their intelligence.

Joy in the companionship and unswerving support they've given me, in the good times and the bad times.

Joy and pride, pride and joy, that they are, when all is said and done, just such good kids.

This book is dedicated to my pride and joy:

My two children, Kyle and Rhett.

Acknowledgments

To all the people whose ideas, input, encouragement, and experience helped me to make this book a reality: Michelle, Eli, John, Alison, Don and Cindy, Dustin, Pat, Spencer, Jennifer, Hunter, Malla, Mom, Herb, Eric, Ruby, Karen, Arthur, Granny Jewel, Trevor, Whitney, Max, Jason, Dana; to the people who called and told stories of childhood entrepreneurism in response to an appeal over Doug's radio show, to Rachel, Matt, Patrick, to my Oprah families, to my kids from One to One, to the folks from the Prodigy Housewife Writers Board (especially Jan), to Beth, Irv, Barb, Bruce, Andy, Martha, Victoria, Julianna, Sue and Dan.

To Valerie Mankoff, noted child psychologist, and Sue Walker, my child care consultant, for their advice and support.

To Sydny Miner, Peter Ginsberg, Eric Martins, George Hitzik, Mark Gompertz, and Marilyn Abraham, without whose efforts this book would never have made it through to fruition.

Contents

Introduction   11
   Before We Start   21
   Defining Your Goals   26
   Our Rules   31

Part One
Preschoolers   35
   Money as a Life Skill   37
   To Market, To Market   45
   Your Preschooler and Values   58

Part Two
School Age   69

Introduction   71
   For Older Children: A Review   72
   Expanding the Jar System   73
   Family Meetings   77
   Family Banking   92
   Work for Pay and Your School-ager   103
   Citizen of the Household Chores and Odd Jobs 110
   Labor and Management   117
   Need Vs. Want   122
   Contracts: Borrowing, Lending, and Trading 129
   Giving and Receiving   136
   Citizen of the Community   148
   The Smart Consumer   157
   Career Development   166
   Watch Those Messages You're Sending!   170

Part Three
Teenagers   175
  Smooth and Painless?   177
  Welcome to the Planet Earth   181
  Expanding Money Skills   190
  Before They Leave the Nest   195
  Budgeting   201
  Phasing Out   207
  Investments   214
  Facing the World   219
  Consequences of Actions   228

Epilogue: Out the Door   233

Index   235

Introduction

Why me?

What makes a banker qualified to write a book about child rearing?

I've asked myself the same question, ever since people started asking me to write this book. And people started asking me to write this particular book around the time I appeared on *The Oprah Winfrey Show* in February 1994. I had done the show the previous November, with a group of families who were rapidly becoming dysfunctional because of their inability to handle money.

The families who most caught the audience's attention were the ones with children. Back in November these families were drowning in debt. One couple had spent $2,500 on Christmas for their kids, which put them into heavy debt for the rest of the year. In fact, that was their pattern every year.

The other couple was mortgaging their future to build a new wing on their house as a fantasy playworld for the kids, complete with stereos, TVs, computers, and their own refrigerator. The parents seemed to think it was the way it had to be. "I give them things because they're things I wish I had when I was a kid," said the mother of two. "If it makes them happy, it makes me happy." But were they happy? They seemed pleased . . . but not satisfied. Would giving them more satisfy them? The other parents—of six children!—echoed the same thought: "The kids would be a lot happier if they could have all the things that their friends do. . . . We've gone into debt to meet those needs."

But did the kids really need all that? The parents said yes . . . they wouldn't be popular unless they had all this stuff. Oprah's audience didn't seem to think so. They were downright hostile to these "spoiled, greedy" kids—and the other kids in the audience were just as hostile as the adults! Oprah asked me if I would work with them—put them on budgets, try to develop healthy spending and saving habits. The families agreed to work with me, and I spent four months with these families. We returned to Oprah in February.

The families and—most of all—the children had turned themselves around. If they had seemed like selfish, acquisitive little brats in November, now they were nice! More than that, they felt better about themselves. They had stuck to their budgets, they had pitched in with the household chores, and they had become responsible citizens of a newly responsible family.

And I began to realize that, yes, the lessons of budgeting, the lessons of financial responsibility, the lessons I wrote about in my last book, *Money Doesn't Grow on Trees: A Parent's Guide to Raising Financially Responsible Children,* really did apply to life's other issues. Teaching your children about value was a sound basis for teaching them about values and about the way the world really works.

In many ways this book is an extension of those workshops that were represented by my two Oprah families, whom I came to love and admire for their courage in admitting their problems and their perseverance in addressing them.

During the time I was vice president of The Chase Manhattan Bank, president of The First Women's Bank, and member of the board of directors of UNICEF, I was also a mother. No, let me rephrase that. Once my first child was born, I was a mother first—like all of us, first, last, and always. I was a mother in a variety of households—first as part of a nuclear family, then as a single mom.

And as long as I've been a parent, I've studied how financial awareness can help shape responsible kids. I created The First Children's Bank at FAO Schwarz, and that led in time to my leaving the world of commercial banking altogether, to found the Children's Financial Network, which is dedicated to teaching children and their parents about money.

Money Is a Tool

Through years of working with children, working with money, raising my own children to be financially responsible, one insight became clearer and clearer to me: The lessons of financial exchange can be applied to social exchange.

Teaching children about money is not teaching about greed or teaching them to become soulless, grasping little Ebenezer Scrooges. Money is about values, about relationships, about choices, about self-esteem. The same dollar that's used to buy drugs can be used to give to charity. The whined-for candy bar or comic book, either given or withheld from the mysterious bottomless well of Mommy's or Daddy's pocket, can be earned money, allotted for a bicycle or for college, and the spoiled (but ultimately helpless) child becomes an empowered partner in his/her own choices.

Money is always a social issue; it never exists in isolation. You can

get it.
save it.
spend it.
share it.

You can't get it alone; you have to make a social contract with someone else and then fulfill your end of that contract. You can't spend it alone; you have to go back into society and make decisions—and if you have a finite amount of money, and you understand that, you have a better chance of making those decisions based on a mature assessment of the value of things. You can save it alone, but that's an intermediate step—the period of quiet contemplation and self-examination that's a necessary part of any social exchange. Giving it means understanding how much you can afford to share and then sharing it with a socially valuable cause. You can choose to save the whales, give to UNICEF, or tithe to your church. Whatever your cause is, charitable giving returns to a sense of self-worth and a sense of connection to your community.

You can get money in bad ways—you can steal it, you can ask for handouts (and sometimes get them). You can spend money in bad ways, which is spending it on junk and spending more than you have. You can save it in bad ways, by hoarding it. You can even give it away in bad ways, if you're trying to buy popularity.

For better or worse, money is the connective tissue that holds society together.

Things Are Different Today

Many of us developed our first worldview in the era of Donna Reed, where the rules were simple. When we grew up, we'd have a house with a picket fence and 2.5 children, there'd always be two parents for every household, mommies would cook gourmet meals, wearing white gloves, and all our children would be able to afford to go to college. How far we are from that world now is shown by the Judds' song, "Grandpa, Tell Me 'bout the Good Old Days," where one of the youngster's questions to Grandpa is, "Did daddies really never go away?"

Many of us were flung from Donna Reed's world into Abbie Hoffman's. There, all rules were bad, and money was a curse. (This was a lot easier to believe in an era of prosperity, where you could drop out of society and still get back in with nothing more than a few years lost. If you got in trouble, your parents could probably bail you out.) The next stop from there was the world of J. R. Ewing, the go-go greed culture, where money became too important in frivolous ways, and the slogan was, "Whoever dies with the most toys wins."

None of those worlds exist anymore. Today, and in the foreseeable future, we live in a society where very few of the old rules about money apply. More than ever we need to understand the new rules and teach our children how to live by them.

The new rules stem from one inescapable fact: The American dream of the post–World War II era is dead. That means you *have* to change your way of looking at money. You can no longer assume that you'll be able to buy the house with the picket fence, that one of you (probably the one who looks most like Donna) will be able to stay home and cook biscuits from scratch, that you'll be able to afford college for your kids, and that your kids will grow up to do better financially than you did.

Today 50 percent of American marriages end in divorce, which means the nuclear family is no longer the norm. Single parenting brings a whole new set of problems, economic and otherwise; stepfamilies create yet another set.

Seventy percent of women with children work outside the home.

It's harder to get money. With major corporations downsizing (a polite way of saying firing lots of perfectly good employees), there's less job stability. Most people can't count on staying with one employer until retirement and the gold watch; in fact, the norm today is not only multiple jobs, but multiple careers. Dr. John Marburger, outgoing president of the State University of New York at Stony Brook, told his 1994 graduates in a commencement address, "The continuity of education and career that many of my classmates experienced is rare today . . . [The future is a field] for which no curriculum seems adequate."*

You can't rely on debt the way you used to be able to. It's riskier to get into . . . and loans are harder to get. Real estate values have gone down, so even if you own your own home, you may not have the kind of equity in it that you thought you had. And this can be a double bind, because the downsizing by traditional employers has created more entrepreneurs and more cottage industries, while making it harder for them to get started.

Moreover, while you may have worked your way through college, that may well be an impossibility for your children. Current estimates have it that for a child born today, a Harvard education will cost close to *$400,000.*

It certainly *feels* as though the world is a lot more dangerous today. I know that parents throughout recorded history have felt that their children were growing up in a more dangerous world than they did, but the proliferation of easy access to drugs and guns, and the specter of AIDS are enough to send chills down the spines of every parent I know.

Certainly there are more high-stress situations today than ever before, by every yardstick we have of gauging stress—losing a job, changing careers, buying and selling a home, moving, divorce, college financing. It's also certain that choices are more complicated today, because we live in an age of television, videos, computers, the information superhigh-

The New York Times, May 16, 1994. One thing is certain: your kids are going to need education, and plenty of it. Here's an estimate from the Hudson Institute's Bureau of Labor Statistics on the amount of education—measured in levels of language, math, and reasoning skills—that will be needed for jobs in the future:

	Current Jobs	New Jobs
8 years or fewer	6%	4%
1–3 years of high school	12%	10%
4 years of high school	40%	35%
1–3 years of college	20%	22%
4 years of college or more	22%	30%

way . . . the age of an information glut. I'll be talking later in this chapter about applying some key concepts of economics to the teaching of values in the household, but let me suggest one right here—Gresham's law, which states that if you have good money and worthless money in circulation at the same time, the worthless money will proliferate and devalue the good money. The same can be true when there's a glut of information—you have to spend all your time simply processing it, and there's no time to sort it out and reflect on its value.

This means, unfortunately, that there may simply not be as much time available for parents to teach values—or for children to learn them. My Oprah families seemed incredibly dysfunctional to a lot of people who watched the show and easy to make fun of—surely we "normal people" aren't anything like that! But they weren't so far outside the norm, really. They were just unusually articulate and honest about what most of us feel to one degree or another: that money can buy happiness, even if means going into debt; that sometimes it's easier to buy the kids designer jeans than to listen to them kvetch about being the only kids in school who don't have them. In a junk information culture, it's easy to settle for fast-food values—we're all guilty of being McMom and McDad, giving in when the whining starts in the supermarket and buying the Double Stuf Oreos.

The great thing about money as an organizer for a value system is that it's efficient and it's constant. It can have different and powerful emotional overtones, but in a basic and important way, it means the same to everyone, and that makes it an understandable system of communication.

I've kept in touch with my Oprah families, and they're staying on their budgets. They tell me they can do it because they finally have the tools and the framework to construct the life they really want and, above all, rules that are *fair* to everyone.

What Kids Don't Know *Can Hurt Them*

Everyone is afraid that their kids are going to grow up with screwed-up values. This is common to almost every family, regardless of its socioeconomic level. You want your kids to grow up with self-esteem, with sound judgment, with self-discipline and the ability to take care of themselves—it doesn't matter what career you or your kids choose, this is true across the board.

There's nothing that you use more than money. You have a constant day-to-day interaction with it that requires continual decision making. You're never not making financial decisions—and if you're not making them on the basis of knowledge, you're making them on the basis of ignorance.

If you don't know the real value of money, you can come to worship it too much. It's very tempting for kids today to see the quick bucks and flashy power displays of drug dealers.

What kids don't know about money *can* hurt them. Bad financial habits in childhood can lead to worse problems when you're grown-up. Too much debt can cripple a family—90 percent of all divorces are traceable to money issues. It can put you in a hole you'll never get out of—from losing your credit rating (from which you can never completely recover, regardless of what anyone tells you) to losing your home. If you don't know the value of money, you can get swindled easily—it happens all the time.

Teaching your kids to have a good grasp on the financial realities is one of the best ways of preparing them to deal with all the unexpected changes life will send their way. Life isn't fair. We all know that, yet it's still a shock every time we're confronted by its unfairness—we need to be solidly grounded so that we're not emotionally devastated.

Relationships to other people are always connected to money. That doesn't mean money is more important than love or friendship, or that people can be bought or sold—just that it's always there and always an object lesson in fairness or unfairness. Money is part of the parent-child relationship, from pay for chores to clothing allowances to college tuition. Money is not only a key part of male-female relationships, misunderstandings over it are the chief cause of divorce. Naturally, it's at the heart of every business or employer-employee relationship, and it figures in friendships as well, from transactions as simple as "Who pays for lunch?" to the sometimes bewildering borrowing and lending that goes on between school-age kids and their friends.

Understanding what money *does* is the first step in understanding what it doesn't do—the first step in teaching your children not to confuse self-worth with net worth. The one who dies with the most toys doesn't win, and no one ever lay on his or her deathbed, moaning, "I wish I had more money in the bank."

How This Book Works

This book is intended for parents-to-be, or parents with kids of any age, who know that a value structure is important and want to teach it to their kids but aren't quite sure where to start or how to go about it.

It *is* hard to know where to start these days. We live in a multicultural society, with different philosophies, different rules, different cultural and religious and regional and generational values. Money is actually one of the few things we have in common—and more than that, it's so *tangible*. Everyone knows exactly what it is and what it measures.

The basic rule that is found throughout every culture, in one form or another, is "Do unto others as you would have them do unto you." This has come to be known as the Golden Rule—a rule as solid as gold. Like gold, it can be used as a measurement . . . a measurement of human virtue, a measurement of values.

As I've lectured over the years and taught courses about parents and kids handling money, I've spent a lot of time thinking about the larger applications of these lessons. And I believe they can be applied, step by step. The first step means that parents or parents-to-be must assess their own money-handling profile. Next, parents must work with their children to teach them money as a life skill. And with that in place, they can use a system of financial responsibility as the basic structure for a value system.

The book is divided into three sections—"Preschoolers," "School Age," and "Teenagers." Child development, of course, goes through many more stages than these, but this isn't a book on child development, and these three units are a good breakdown for a three-stage approach to our subject.

If your child is already older than preschool when you begin the program—even if your child is already a teenager—there's no need to feel discouraged. Just start with the more basic exercises and keep working forward.

Each chapter of the book will begin with practical and theoretical information. Then we'll move on to an interactive session—worksheets, quizzes, and games to involve you and your children in the basics of financial responsibility. Finally, where it's applicable, I'll give you a list of resources beyond this book that may help you to look further into some of the ideas I've introduced you to.

How important is this sort of information to people? I wondered, too, and when George Ravich of PRODIGY Service talked to me about using Prodigy to take a survey of people's family economics knowledge, I thought it sounded like a great idea—if it would work.

"Will enough people respond to give us a reasonable database, George?" I asked. "It won't tell us much unless we get at least a couple of hundred responses."

"I can't promise anything," George said. "We won't be able to advertise it, like we do most of our surveys. And we'll only be able to keep it on-line for eleven days, instead of the full month we normally run a survey."

We agreed that we'd try it. Prodigy ran our questionnaire for its eleven days, and then George called to tell me he was sending me the results.

"Did we get the two hundred responses?" I asked.

"Neale," he said, "we got over thirty-four thousand."

I was convinced. People do want to talk about family finances, and they do want to learn more about how to discuss finances with their children.

Here are some of the highlights of the survey:

	Yes	No
When I was growing up, I knew how much my father made per year.	23%	77%
I knew how much my family's mortgage/rent payment was.	30%	70%
I knew what kind of insurance coverage my family had.	23%	77%
I knew how much it cost to outfit me for grade school.	26%	74%
I would like my children to understand more about financial realities.	91%	9%
I would like to understand better how to educate my children about money.	73%	27%

Before We Start

The value of money as a basis for the teaching of values comes with its own little problems. For example, once you get into talking about the value of money, you find yourself in the middle of a thicket of words that economists or financial planners may understand but the rest of us likely will find bewildering. So in this chapter we're going to look at a few basic financial terms and try to give you some usable definitions for them—definitions you can use in the field of handling money and ones that you can apply further, into other areas of decision making and broader areas of your life.

We'll start with *budgeting*, which is certainly a term we're all far too familiar with. A budget is one of those things no one can quite seem to manage to live within.

But let's look at it a little more closely. The better you understand how a budget works—and the more clearly you understand just how important it is to you and to your children—the more likely you are to be able to stick with it.

In simplest terms, a budget is *money in, money out*. You have a certain amount of money coming in, and you can determine what it is. Salaries are easy. Commissions or income from investment may vary, but you can put a conservative figure to them, a minimum that you can use for totaling the amount of money you can count on coming in. To stick to a budget, you have to make sure you don't have any more money going out than coming in. So far, it's as simple as that.

When you're dividing up your budget, figuring all the different directions the money will be going out, you come up against another financial concept: *fixed* and *variable expenses*.

Fixed expenses, in business accounting, are those that you can't do without and can't change. Basic raw materials for a product are a fixed expense; electricity is a fixed expense. Variable expenses, like research and development, can be extremely important, even vital, to the success of a business. But they have to be measured out according to the total budget.

Households have fixed and variable expenses, too, and so do individuals within those households. In fact, this is one of the most important concepts we'll be dealing with in this book, in a variety of different ways.

Shelter—your mortgage or your rent—is a fixed expense. So is food, and clothing, and transportation, and your kids' education. Pretty much everything else is variable, and even within those fixed categories there's room for discussion. Transportation is a fixed expense—if you live in the suburbs or in the country, you need a car. But you don't necessarily need a new Mercedes, although you may want one. That's *need vs. want,* and we'll be talking about it over and over again, and both concepts can apply to the same purchase.

Once you have the concept clear, and you've shown your family how it's applied—and shown them *that* it will be applied—you can relate it to behavior, too. You can have—and you should write them out, just as you write out your fixed and variable expenses when you're making up a household budget—*negotiable and nonnegotiable rules of conduct,* rules that can be discussed and perhaps modified if the kids can convince you of their point of view, as well as rules that are absolute and not open for discussion.

"Fixed" sounds like an immutable concept, and it is, for the most part—but even here there's some room for judgment calls. A college education is a fixed expense in our family; in some others it may not be. I plan on sending Kyle (who's now in middle school) and Rhett (who's in grade school) to college, and that's part of my budget.

Here's a quiz for the whole family to take. I've thrown together a list, in alphabetical order, of things that families might spend money on. Which ones are fixed expenses, and which ones are variable? Take the quiz separately, then compare answers and discuss the ones you've answered differently from each other. Why the difference? What's the logic for your choice?

Car	Plumbing
Cocoa Puffs	Private school
College for kids	Rec room
College for Mom or Dad	Refrigerator
Country club	Romance novels
Designer jeans	Schoolbooks
Extra bedroom	Sound system
Food	Stove
House payments	Summer camp
Medical school	Telephone
Mercedes	Tennis lessons
Nose job	TV

You may find that everyone's choices are a little different. Chances are you'll agree on certain basics—food, shelter, clothing. Beyond that, what is absolutely necessary? A businessperson parent might include the country club dues—perhaps some very important business contacts are inextricably tied to the golf course. A new stove? The parent most responsible for kitchen duty will know you need one before anyone else does. Tennis lessons? Suppose one of the kids has real talent, and tennis lessons can mean a college scholarship?

The point is, the concept of fixed vs. variable—or necessary vs. unnecessary—expenses can be a straightforward one in business but a lot more subtle for a family. It's important, for our kids and ourselves, to create a sensible framework, a solid context to which we can relate our value judgments. Ultimately these are the bases for many of our most important life choices.

Penny Wise, Pound Foolish

Speaking of putting college in your budget, one thing we all know is how the cost of a college education has skyrocketed and continues to skyrocket. I could work my way through college; for my kids, no matter how much ambition and initiative they have, it won't be possible. So when we talk about budgeting and determining our fixed and variable expenses, we have to add another concept to the mix: *goal setting.* There's a bigger picture here, and if you don't take it into account, sometimes penny wise can be pound foolish. Your budget can't be just what you're spending week to week or month to month; it also has to include *short-term* and *long-term goals*—what you'll need (and what you'll want) five years from now . . . or fifteen or twenty years from now.

One of the most important tools you can bring to bear on goal setting is a financial concept called *time value of money.* This one's a little more difficult, but getting it straight can give you a tremendous advantage in setting your goals, making and sticking to a budget, winning the never-ending battle of mind over money.

Essentially, time value of money is a way of answering the question "What's the best way to ensure that the purchasing power of your money is going to be greater in the future?" In business this can be very complicated stuff, depending on a whole lot of variables. For instance, if you take out a five-year loan for $3,791, at 8 percent interest, and invest it in a business that makes $1,000 a year, at the end of five years you'll have paid off the loan and have $296 to the good. If you sell the business for $202 as soon as you take out the loan and invest the money at 8 percent interest, at the end of five years you'll have exactly the same amount: $296.*

For the rest of us, it doesn't have to be worked out in such detail, but the point is to make your money work for you so you come out ahead of the game. Is your money working better for you if you buy a small house rather than a larger, invest the difference, and five years later sell the small house and buy the larger one? Or should you invest now in the house you're going to need five years from now when your family is larger and pay those larger mortgage payments every month?

Benjamin Franklin left a legacy that's a testimony to the time value of

*Charles Horngren, *Cost Accounting: A Managerial Emphasis,* Prentice-Hall, 1977.

money: when he died in 1791, he left the city of Boston $5,000, with the stipulation that it could not be spent for one hundred years but should be left to accumulate interest. By 1891 Franklin's $5,000 had grown to $400,000. At that time, a little over $300,000 was withdrawn to build a school. The city left the remaining $92,000 where it was, to continue to accrue interest.

The account is now worth over a million dollars.

Time value of money is another concept that you can use in many ways in your everyday life. It's a really good way of teaching children the value of saving. You and your child can sit down with a pencil and paper, or a computer, or a stack of coins for a younger child, and the two of you can figure out the best way to make money work. Use your imagination!

Problem solving is the best kind of empowerment. And this is a key first step in developing a child's skills at *deferred gratification,* the ability to understand and accept that putting off an immediate satisfaction can lead to greater satisfaction down the line. This is one of the most important money skills, and life skills, that you can learn.

You can apply it, as well, to budgeting your time and energy. There's a time value of time as well: is your time worth more than what it will cost you to get someone else to do a job? (This doesn't mean, of course, that your eight-year-old entrepreneur can hire someone to clean his/her room—there's another time value of time that takes precedence here, and that has to do with learning the basic life skill of being responsible for yourself and your surroundings.)

Defining Your Goals

What are you hoping to get out of this book? Before you go any farther, you should take a look at your own financial personality and take stock of yourself. The first lessons, and most of the important lessons that children learn, are from their parents, not from books—especially in an area that's as emotionally sensitive as our attitudes toward money.

Right now those are perhaps the most emotionally sensitive attitudes we have. In the 1970s and 1980s, with the help of books, TV and radio talk shows, and a general shift in public perceptions, many people became less ashamed of their sexuality, and that was a good thing. Now, people will go on talk shows and talk about cross-dressing, about their bedroom secrets, about carrying on simultaneous affairs with triplets, but if you ask them how much money they make a year, they'll pull back and say, "That's *personal*."

So answer the questions on this quiz as honestly as you can, remembering that you're not going to be graded on it or held against some unrealistic standard of perfection—not that such a thing even exists. We grow up with ideas about money that we got from our parents, and we pass them on to our kids. We may not want to pass some of them on. They may have worked in our parents' generation but they certainly aren't going to work in the world our children will inherit. Now is the time to make those decisions.

This next worksheet is to help you create a paradigm, a template of your household's financial personality. It's not meant to be judgmental—there's no single right or wrong way to run a household, and you're not being graded on this. It's just designed to help you find out where you are now and how that jibes with the financial paradigm you'd ideally like to see your kids fitting into.

You and Your Money: Taking Stock

Getting

Goal Setting

Who makes decisions as to who works, who stays home?

What is the basis of the decision?

One person to stay home with kids

One person to go to school

Traditional breadwinner attitude

Personal career goals for both parties

Necessity of two incomes

No choice—single-parent family

Other

Whose job takes priority if a move is necessary or desirable?

How It Works Out

Who earns the money in your family?

Male partner

Female partner

Two-income family

Single parent

Are there other sources of income?

Inheritance

Current gifts from in-laws, parents, and the like

Investments

Saving

Goal Setting

Who makes the decisions on goals for which family is saving/investing?

Who makes the investment vehicle decisions?

How much is the decision-making process shared or explained?

Who makes the decisions on the family's insurance goals and strategies?

Who makes the insurance plan decisions?

How much is the decision-making process shared or explained?

How It Works Out

Who does the day-to-day, month-to-month work of investing?

Who handles bank accounts? Who has access to funds?

Who has contacts with the following?

  Financial planners

  Brokers

  Insurance agents

  Accountants

  Lawyers

Spending

Goal Setting

Who makes small-item buying decisions?

  How much and what kind of input from other family members?

Who makes large-item buying decisions?

  How much and what kind of input from other family members?

How It Works Out

Who does the small-item buying?

Who does the large-item buying?

Who's in charge of the weekly household budget?

Who picks out and purchases gifts?

Sharing within the Household

Goal Setting

Who sets goals as to sharing what comes in?

How It Works Out

Do you have joint or separate accounts?

Is your house owned jointly? How does the title read?

Who has title to your car(s)?

How are household responsibilities divided?

  Kitchen chores

  Cleaning chores

  Repairing chores

  Child care chores (including finding day care or sitters)

Yardwork
Gardening
Other
How is disposable income apportioned?
Who makes decisions about family time?
  Vacations
  Entertainment/eating out
  Day trips/outings
  Holidays with relatives
  Other

Sharing in the Larger Community
Goal Setting
Who sets goals as to charitable sharing?

How It Works Out
Who makes decisions about charitable/religious giving?
  What charity?
  How much?
Who makes decisions about giving time to socially conscious/religious activities?
  What activity?
  How much?

Now, which of these patterns do you want to pass on to your children and which ones do you hope they'll avoid?

Think about this: If you've fallen into patterns that are not what you'd want your children to be learning, maybe they aren't really the best ones for you to be in, either. One of the best times to take stock of ourselves is precisely at this time: when we're thinking about what we want for our children.

On the other hand, some of the patterns in your life may work for you but nevertheless may not fit into the brave new world of the twenty-first century. For many households of your parents' generation, the mom-staying-home-with-the-kids paradigm worked very well indeed. It's no criticism of Grandma to say that it's no longer the only paradigm for a contemporary mother, that, in fact, it's not even the principal one.

If there are patterns you're satisfied with for yourself, but you don't want to make your children think they're expected to follow them, it's best to know what they are so that you can talk about them.

What Kind of Child Do You Want?

All this relates directly to thinking about just what kind of children you want to have. My Oprah families shocked millions of people when they said they wanted their children to have consumer goods that they themselves had not gotten as kids; but what they really meant (as they came to understand) was that they wanted their kids to have the happiness, self-confidence, and stability that had been missing from their own childhoods.

We want our children to do better than we did. For generations of American life, we've been accustomed to measuring that in terms of material success, and we want our children to be financially stable. But that's just a small part of a larger package. What we really want—what we're really working toward, in this book and in all of our efforts—is to raise children who are happy, healthy, self-sufficient, well rounded, secure, and ultimately independent—able to make good life' decisions both professionally and personally. Isn't that what it's all about?

Our Rules
or

When in Rome, Do As the Romans Do

Your financial patterns, and your rules for the way money is spent, saved, and budgeted, are not going to be the only ones in the world, and they're not going to be the only ones your kids come in contact with. As soon as they reach the age of socialization and start playing with other kids, they're going to start being affected by peer pressure. "Everyone else's parents," as your kids will invariably see it, have the permissiveness of Timothy Leary, the resources of Donald Trump, and the generosity of Santa Claus.

There are two simple answers to this one. The first one, which you can't really give (though sometimes you may want to) is, "Fine, go live with them." The second, more appropriate one, is that every family has different rules, and these are yours. (P.S. If you do choose the first response, it won't do your kids any good—everyone else's parents aren't really like that.)

One of the most difficult situations to deal with is divorced-household rules. If you are divorced, it's most likely that you and your ex don't see eye to eye on all sorts of things. Since money is at center of the overwhelming percentage of divorces, there's a strong chance you and your ex don't see eye to eye on theories of handling money.

If the divorce is amicable, or at least civil, it's *extremely* important to talk these differences through and try to get on the same wavelength as much as possible. Give your ex a copy of this book, then sit down with him/her and see how many of its principles and techniques you can agree on.

If you and your ex aren't speaking to each other above a hiss, or if, with the best will in the world, you have disagreements on money issues, then you just have to accept it and make it clear to your children: "These are our rules, and in this house they are the rules we live by. Daddy may give you a quarter every time you go to the potty or a dollar every time you clean up your room [or Mommy may agree that a nine-year-old *has* to have a pair of Air Jordans that glow in the dark], but those aren't our rules." We're always going to think that our rules are the sound ones, and that vile creature we split up with is the one with the potentially ruinous values, but mostly that's not true. The best attitude here is nonjudgmental—there are two sets of rules, and in your house you set the rules.

Finally, there are grandparents. Freud said, somewhere or other, that every time a couple goes to bed there are at least four other people in bed with them—his parents and her parents. The same is certainly true every time you open your wallet, only worse. Your parents aren't *really* going to climb into bed with you, but they may really be standing there, looking over your shoulder and second-guessing you every time you open that wallet. And they're almost certainly going to have different rules from yours—quite likely including spoiling the kids the way they never spoiled you.

Fortunately this is not too much of a problem. Grandparents are special, and kids know it instinctively. There are Grandma rules—maybe you dress a little more formally when you visit Grandma, maybe you talk a little more quietly. The rewards that Grandma and Grandpa give you are because you're extraspecial to them, and they represent a situation that doesn't exist anywhere else in real life.

There are a couple of exceptions here. If you're living in an extended family situation, with three generations under the same roof, then Grandma rules and "our" rules may come into conflict, and these conflicts have to be worked out.

If grandparents give an exceptionally large amount of money—a birthday or Christmas or Bar Mitzvah gift that is exponentially out of line with the amount of money your child normally gets at one time—you are within your rights to bring this under the "our" rules jurisdiction and insist that the lion's share of it goes into the savings account. (I'll be dealing with gifts in detail in a later chapter.)

After all, we're teaching our children to be adaptable, to live in a world that has a plethora of value systems—different households, different schools, different corporations, different countries with different laws and customs. When in Rome, do as the Romans do. And if your house is Rome, Italy, and your ex's is Rome, New York, this is as good a place as any to start.

Part One
Preschoolers

Money as a Life Skill

Magic Plastic Cards and Little Silver Coins

The first things little children learn about money are (a) it can get them things they want; and (b) their parents always seem to have it. In fact, if we're not careful, money can take on a magical quality to them. When Rhett was three, we were out together one day, and he saw a toy he wanted. Naturally he asked me to buy it for him.

I told him I didn't have any money with me—which was true. Like any other parent, I'm capable of saying the first thing that comes into my head in certain moments of weakness, but I never lie about money. Too much missionary zeal, I guess.

"Oh, don't worry, Mommy," he said. "You can just use that magic plastic card you carry in your purse."

That taught me a few things—not the least of which was the resourcefulness of a small child bent on getting what he wants. It also brought home to me the necessity of making sure that even our little ones begin learning the value of money.

Little children's first natural instincts are for survival. The first concept they're going to understand—the first one they *need* to understand—is getting; and after that comes having. When it comes to money, they're naturally going to understand spending first, earning second. A true understanding of saving and sharing doesn't come till later. But it's still important that parents keep presenting all four aspects of dealing with money together, as a natural part of the process.

Magic card or no, it's the tangibility of money that makes it such an effective early tool in teaching children how the world is structured. It's tangible and it's visible: they see it every day, they see it being used, and they quickly grasp the general concept of how it's used. (As a matter of fact, Rhett was right and I was wrong in that toy store—I did have money in the form of my little plastic card. I explained to him about the card: it didn't mean I got things for free or by magic; it was a promise to pay the money at the end of the month. I also had to simply tell him no, I wasn't going to buy him that toy, on that day.)

Money is *one* of the first experiences a child has with abstract, symbolic concepts. Speech is the first, and that may well be the hardest intellectual challenge a human being faces—understanding that these strange sounds big people make actually represent things, and actions, and even feelings you can't see like hunger or sleepiness, happiness or sadness.

If a child can work that one out, she can work out that silver coins and green pieces of paper—if they're the right ones—can be exchanged for things she really wants, like toys and candy.

If you ask your children what Mommy and Daddy do with money, and they can answer, "They go into the store and buy things with it," then they have grasped the basic concept of using money as a medium of exchange.

The truth is, I can't know exactly what Rhett was thinking or what magic he imagined in that little card. But he did know you had to do *something*—you couldn't just walk into the store and take the toy away with you.

Susan Walker, who operates a day care center in Kingston, New York, and who has provided this book with some wonderful insights on working with preschoolers, has seen her two-year-old, Patrick, learn his first lessons about money at a local game arcade. "He knows Mommy turns in the green pieces of paper for coins, and that you can put coins into slots to make the games work," she says. "In fact, that's why I had to get the seat belts in my car fixed. Patrick put a quarter in the slot of the seat belt fastener."

Show and Tell

The first lessons to teach your child are built around games that encourage a tangible relationship to money. They are money identification games, stacking and counting games, change-making games, measuring games.

For all of these games, use real money, not play money. Toddlers have been known to swallow coins. Supervise your children closely and take the money away when you are finished playing.

Money Identification Games

These are the basic games, the first ones you'll teach (although variations on money bingo can make it a favorite for a few years, anyway). Very little children won't fully understand concepts of value at first, but they can understand games of "how much." They must be able to see, and be able to identify, the physical substance of money before they can do anything with it.

The Coin Identification Game

Goal: To tell the difference between one coin and another.

You'll need: Four jars, each of them marked with all the names of the coin that jar will represent. The penny jar will be labeled *"Penny, 1¢, One Cent"*; the nickel jar *"Nickel, 5¢, Five Cents"*; the dime jar *"Dime, 10¢, Ten Cents"*; the quarter jar *"Quarter, 25¢, Twenty-five Cents."* Put a few coins of the right denomination in each jar.

You'll also need a *dish* and a *bunch of coins* of different denominations.

Rules: First, pick up a coin from the dish, tell the child what it is ("penny," "nickel," and so on), and have the child repeat the name of the coin and put it in the right jar. Next, you can add another challenge by naming the coin and asking the child to give the other name for it ("quarter," "twenty-five cents").

When he has mastered that round, tell him the name of the coin and have him find it in the dish and put it in the right jar.

What it teaches: Recognizing different coins by appearance, identifying them by name. Since the jars are picked up and put away at the end of each game session, it also teaches neatness and responsibility for belongings. And the sorting of money into jars for fun gives the child an early positive feeling about the jars he'll be using later on for saving.

Money Bingo

Goal: To fill up a "bingo card"; if you're playing with more than one child, to be the first to fill up a bingo card.

You'll need: "Bingo cards" that you make up yourself, on pieces of cardboard, so they can be reused. Each card has twenty-five circles on it, five rows of five circles. You make the circles by tracing around coins—pennies, nickels, dimes, and quarters—and then writing the value of each coin in the center of the circle. Write it in numerals—25¢, 5¢, and so forth. Make different cards, with the circles in different orders, with different numbers of each coin—three nickels and eight quarters on one, five nickels and six quarters on the next, and so on.

You'll need a pile of coins for each child.

Rules: You hold up a coin and say its name, not its value (penny, nickel, dime, or quarter). Each child has to fill all the circles on his or her card with a coin in the right denomination. After four rounds, the one who has filled the most spaces wins. If all the children fill up their whole cards, everyone wins.

What it teaches: In addition to coin identification, this is the very beginning of another important life lesson. Exchange of money for goods is a life skill that is always performed under pressure. When you buy something, you have to come up with at least the right amount of money and give it to someone who is judging your ability to handle this task. There's time pressure, too—this other person expects you to do it promptly. If you give more than the right amount of money, you'll get change back, and you have to count that quickly and make sure it's right. These are skills that can be daunting to children, and the play pressure of money bingo can help get them used to it.

Further variations: Have the children make their own game cards, by doing soft pencil or crayon rubbings of coins. This makes another game—the rubbings themselves—and also a fun new complication to the bingo game itself. The children then have to identify the coin you've called out by the image on the rubbing—and it can be either heads or tails. For older preschoolers and younger school-age kids, this can make the game even more like real bingo, if they have to identify the side of the coin and the color of the rubbing. For example: "Orange quarter—tails!"

Counting, Stacking, and Change-Making Games

Counting and stacking moves the child along into the conceptual side of money—beginning to relate it to the idea of value—first in relation to itself and then in relation to things. Change making extends this concept and adds a little more challenging arithmetic.

Once you start on these conceptual games, you are beginning to teach lessons of fair exchange, which is the underpinning of any system of values.

What's It Worth?

Goal: Find out how many smaller-denomination coins go into a larger-denomination coin or a dollar bill.

You'll need: Coins and bills.

Rules: Put down a penny. Explain that it's worth one cent. Put down a nickel. Explain that it's worth five cents, and that you can call it either by its value (five cents) or it's name (a nickel). Have your child count out enough pennies to make one nickel. Do the same with dimes (ten pennies, two nickels) and so on, up to a dollar.

What it teaches: In addition to counting skills, it helps the child understand the symbolic value of money—that this one coin—a quarter, for example—is worth the same amount as twenty-five pennies.

Further variations: This lesson can be reinforced by bringing your child to the store with you and letting him buy an item with twenty-five pennies, and then the next day letting him buy the same item with a quarter.

The Price Tag Game: 1

Goal: Match the item to its price.

You'll need: Canned or packaged goods with price tags on them; piles of coins of different denominations.

Rules: The child reads the price on the item—with your help, if necessary. Then she takes coins from the piles and stacks them next to the item until she has matched the amount. Then the money goes back into the piles. You'll start with simple items—something costing a quarter will only need one coin; something costing twelve cents will need a minimum of three; but the counting is still pretty simple. Gradually you can work up to more expensive items that will further challenge the child's counting abilities.

What it teaches: The relationship of money to goods.

Further variations: Change the items, or add new items, each time you play the game. Use both household items (a bar of soap) and "kid items" (stickers). This begins to get the kids noticing the relative value of things. If they mention it ("Daddy, look, a bar of soap costs the same as two candy bars!"), you can talk about what a bar of soap does and how long it lasts, compared to two candy bars.

The Price Tag Game: 2

Goal: "Buy" different items using a finite amount of money.
You'll need: The same as for price tag 1.
Rules: The child will stack the appropriate number of coins next to an item, just as in the previous game. This time, though, after he has correctly matched the price of one item, he leaves the item and the stack of coins on the table and goes on to another item.
What it teaches: The notion of a finite supply of money—the more you spend, the less you have.
Further variations: You can start with a group of objects and a certain amount of money that adds up to less than the total value of the objects. Make sure the child knows this, so he won't be upset when he runs out. When there's not enough money left, that's the end of a round, and he can start again, this time with a different "purchasing plan."

The Change-Making Game

Goal: Playing store—selling different items, taking the customer's money, and making change.
You'll need: A "cash register" of a shallow box each for pennies, nickels, dimes, quarters, and dollar bills, money for each box, and items to sell in the "store."
Rules: The child gets to set up her own store, with whatever items from around the house she wants to sell. You and she can decide appropriate prices for the items and put price tags on them.

She arranges the change and the dollar bills in the cash register, from left to right in descending order of value.

You come in as the customer, buy something, and bring it up to the "storekeeper." Pay for it with more than the value of the item—a dollar bill or a five-dollar bill, whatever will make it necessary for the storekeeper to give change. She "rings up" the item, figures out your correct change, and gives it to you.

Take turns being customer and storekeeper. When the child is the customer, she must make sure you give her the correct change.

After the game is finished, she must put all the change back in the change jars (see "The Coin Identification Game," page 39).

What it teaches: Giving and receiving correct change. This is also a good groundwork for teaching fairness and honesty. You can talk about what to do if the storekeeper gives you too much change (always correct the mistake). When this lesson is attached to the child's pride in counting right and figuring the change right, the moral lesson is strengthened. Make sure, though, that the child understands the moral consequences—taking money that doesn't belong to you is stealing; the cashier might have to pay for it out of his pocket, or it might even cost him his job.

Further variations: Start buying more than one thing, so that the child has to total up a sum before making the correct change. Have an item marked "three for a dollar" and only buy one—you can explain to the child why the storekeeper would round the price up to thirty-four cents.

Buy too much— more than the money you give the storekeeper will cover. When she points this out to you, the two of you can figure what you would have to put back in order to be able to afford the purchase.

Kitchen Games

Goal: The goals here combine counting and measuring with getting things done around the house.

You'll need: Whatever's at hand in the kitchen—food, bowls, measuring cups and spoons.

Rules: The simplest games here are *Sesame Street*-type counting games: How many hamburger patties are we making? How many forks do we put on the table?

For older children, these become recipe games—actually measuring and combining ingredients to make pancakes or a salad.

What it teaches: Counting games are always good to teach familiarity with numbers and the relationship of numbers to each other and to real life: for example, the number of forks on the table is the same as the number of people in the family! When combined with chores like setting the table, they become part of the child's developing sense of responsibility as a Citizen of the Household.

Recipe games teach measurements—a whole new concept of counting and relating different amounts and values to each other. At the same time, following a simple recipe and making something that can be eaten develops a child's sense of empowerment and the sense that he can make a contribution to society.

Deferred Gratification Games

Very little children are not big on deferred gratification, but you have to start teaching it young. Hiding and finding games are a good way to start teaching this concept—hiding a present somewhere in the living room, giving clues as to where it is, makes not actually getting it right away part of the fun. After that, you can try offering your toddler a choice that will begin to show the advantages of deferred gratification: "Would you rather have one cookie now or two cookies after you've finished playing outside for an hour?" Make sure the time of deferral is very short at first.

It is, however, *not* a good idea to play these games with money. You don't want to encourage the idea of money as something to be hidden and searched for. Remember the classic story of Soupy Sales telling his kid TV audience to go into Mommy and Daddy's room, find all the little pieces of green paper, and send them to Soupy? Soupy was kidding, but he got into trouble for it anyway, and it's best that you also try not to encourage the practice.

To Market, To Market

Trips to the Store

The real world is the best classroom you have. All those games are preparation for money exchanging situations in the real world and visits to the store—the supermarket, the local hardware store, the mall. Little children like to be included, and these are lessons you can repeat over and over again, every time you shop.

First, just talk through the whole process. Talk about what you're doing, what you're shopping for, and what you'll use it for, and talk through the process of paying and change making.

Talk about your budgeting process, too. It won't mean a lot to your little one at first, but it will give both of you an easy, shared experience of talking about money and finances of your household. This kind of interaction can be the icebreaker for a whole lifetime of conversations.

In other words, this is an exercise that really works on two levels. In the first place, you're educating your child about some important money transactions—shopping and budgeting. At the same time you're schooling yourself to break through what, for many of us, are deeply entrenched emotional barriers.

It's hard for us to talk to our children about our own money. I'm no different from anyone else in this area. I grew up in a household where women and children—especially girl children—*never* asked questions about money and never knew anything about family finances. That's been a hard lesson to unlearn. Frankly, when my kids ask what something costs, I still find that I have to suppress a reflex to say, "None of your business." Tad, my collaborator, remembers a hurdle he had to clear when he and his wife, Pat, were first courting. Her eight-year-old son, Dustin, used to want to look at the check every time they went out to a restaurant. "No one in my family would ever have *dreamed* of looking at the check to see how much a meal had cost," he says. "I wanted to tell him, 'Keep your hands to yourself, kid—if you're not paying for the meal, it's none of your business how much it costs.' But some instinct told me to bite my tongue. Maybe this wasn't hopelessly bad manners— maybe he was really learning something about how the world worked.

"And sure enough . . . before long he was totaling up the bill, and even figuring the tax, to make sure we were being charged correctly."

Once you're into the swing of talking about the money you're spending, you can introduce the concept of budgeting. Some people like to budget their money the old-fashioned way, by putting it in kitchen canisters marked "Mortgage" or "Rent," "Groceries," "Electric Bill," and so forth. If you do that, you can actually show them to your child, but if you pay bills by check, or even by Prodigy or some other on-line service of the information superhighway, you can still talk about how you put a certain amount of money aside for groceries each week, and that's all you spend, so you can have enough money for the other things you need to buy and some left over for things you want to buy.

"Shopping Research" Games

You can move on from here, when your youngster is ready for it, to "shopping research" games.

The simplest of these are "finding games"—identification games— and counting and measuring games.

The Finding Game: 1

Goal: To find a list of things that have something in common.
You'll need: To be in a store, preferably one that you know well enough to be able to direct the kids to where they'll find what they're looking for.
Rules: Have your child look for shapes, colors, and textures: How many round things can you find? How many red things? How many rough things?
What it teaches: The basic use for money, the first one your child learns about, is an exchange of symbolic value for actual value—those little green pieces of paper in exchange for things you can eat and drink and wear. So you're laying a solid groundwork for the next round of shopping lessons with these games of observing—finding and counting and measuring—the things that you're exchanging your money for.

The Finding Game: 2

Goal: To find out how much five dollars buys.

You'll need: A store, as in finding game 1.

Rules: Have your child figure out how many items in a certain department she can "buy" for a certain amount of money: how many canned goods for five dollars, how many pairs of underpants for ten dollars?

What it teaches: This is a wonderful arithmetic-learning game, preparing your child for school, and it also emphasizes the application of school lessons to real life. Furthermore, it gets your child used to thinking about what different things cost. If she asks why something that's smaller costs more than something that's bigger, that opens the door for a whole series of simple economics lessons that a child can understand: the differing values of raw materials, the quality of workmanship, even the laws of supply and demand—people are willing to pay more for a jacket that has their favorite baseball team's name on it.

Further variations: When you're buying items that are measured, you can reverse this game—here's a set amount of money, now you have to "buy" the product to fit it. If oranges cost $.98 a half dozen, give her the $.98 and have her count out six oranges; if you're getting half a pound of wood screws at $1.28 a pound, give her the $.64 and have her weigh out the half pound and add or take away screws until she's got exactly the right weight.

The shopping games come next. You've played the change-making games at home—now do them in the store.

The Shopping Game

Goal: To choose an item and figure out how to pay for it and get the right change.

You'll need: To be in a store, but away from the pressure situation of the cash register. Play this game out in the aisles of the store.

Rules: Pick out an item—a pair of socks, say—and help your child find the price on it. Then have her figure out: If you bought these socks and paid for them with a five-dollar bill, how much change would you get back?

After you've done that for a while, and your child is used to figuring these things in the store, the two of you are ready for the next step—a real-life experience. While you're shopping, have your child select something for herself with her own allowance (yes, even your three-year-old—we'll talk about this in the next chapter). Then, with you there to supervise, let her pay for it herself, get the change back, and count the change to make sure it's correct. Then she can have it bagged in her own bag and carry it out to the car by herself.

The first time you try this, it's a good idea to do it in a small store where the owner or clerk knows you and your child.

There's one problem with trying out this game for real: most items in a real store are taxed, so the price that's marked on them won't be the price your child will actually have to pay. There are no wonderful ways around this, but here are a couple you can try.

If you live in a state that has nontaxable items (many states, for example, have no sales tax on produce), make sure (at least for the first couple of buying games) that your child buys one of those nontaxable items.

If you live in a state where everything is taxed, then explain to the child that she will have to pay some extra money for the tax. Later on you'll teach her how to figure the tax herself, but for now you'll just give her the tax money separately. When she pays for the item, she can hand it to the grocer and say, "And this is for the tax."

This is also a good opportunity to explain to your child what taxes are. Young children, and even school-age children, are not going to understand the concept of taxes at all. But they are going to hear about them—and almost always negatively. As adults we understand what taxes do, and depending on our political and economic beliefs, we more or less accept them as a good thing or a necessary evil. But we almost never talk about them except to complain about them, and children do hear that.

I brought this up on *The Oprah Winfrey Show,* where I did one of those classic things you never do on television—count on kids not to be unpredictable—and it worked out for me. I bet Oprah that if she took a kid at random in the audience and asked whether taxes were a good thing or a bad thing, the answer would be "Bad."

I was right. I took a deep breath and thanked the kid for making me look good on television. Most kids, unless they're educated differently, will think that.

After your child has done this a few times and feels secure with the process, you can start letting him figure the tax. Do this at home first, in the context of your home store game.

Figuring tax, of course, involves a multiplication problem, which will be a little too sophisticated for your preschooler (at least at first); but it's not too sophisticated if you start him using a *calculator*. Any child who knows his numbers can learn how to use a calculator.

Bring an item up to the counter of your home store. Put down the money for the purchase (do it in coins first, to make the lesson more visual). Take the calculator. Enter the amount of the purchase. Press the "x." Enter the amount of the tax—".07" for 7 percent for example. Explain to your child what you're doing each step of the way. Explain that the number on the calculator now is the amount of the tax (you can explain rounding off to the left of the decimal point, too). Then put a new pile of money next to the first pile. Your child already knows the concept of a little extra money for the tax. Now he's learning how to figure out how much it is.

Next you can include figuring in the tax in the change-making game. When your child is comfortable with this, you can go back to the store again. This time he'll bring his calculator with him; he'll know how to figure the tax, and he'll be prepared to pay it.

Finally, let him shop by himself (again, his first solo flight is best taken at a small store where your family is known). You can accompany him but let him make his choice and do his figuring by himself. Discuss the whole project with him beforehand, including what he's going to buy and how he's going to figure the tax. Then let him go in and shop and pay for the item by himself and count the change as before. Afterward he can bring back the change and discuss the whole adventure with you.

Your own judgment will tell you when your child is ready for this. Some four-year-olds can do it; other children need to wait till they're five or six. Frankly, there are some sixteen-year-olds I wouldn't send to the store alone.

This is a good time to begin the "need vs. want" game, which is one that will continue, with some variations and added subtleties, throughout your child's development. Actually it changes very little from the way you'll start it out with your preschooler. While you're out shopping, you hold something up and say, "Do we *need* this, or do we *want* it?"

This will be a new and perhaps confusing concept at first; it is one of the very first steps that your child is going to be taking toward growing up—and he'll be taking it at about the age of three.

That's a little early for most of us to be thinking about our babies growing up. But it really is the time that you should be starting to teach your children the lessons of financial responsibility—and time to start them as contributing, wage-earning members of the household. I'll be telling you all about this concept in the next chapter.

The Need vs. Want Game

Goal: To determine whether an item is something you need or something you want.

You'll need: Nothing except your imagination—which is why this is a great car game. It can also be played in a store, where you can actually point to the items you're talking about.

Rules: Someone names an item—either generic or a brand-name item—and everyone has to make a case for whether it's a "need" or a "want." Beyond that, you can make up your own rules—from household to household, sometimes even from one round of the game to another. It can be a structured game, like a formal debate. But even if it's a silly-hilarious game, with hair-splitting, laugh-provoking distinctions, it's still teaching something.

Further variations: For preschoolers, start the need vs. want game with obvious things like hamburger vs. bubble gum, a winter coat vs. a Mighty Ducks baseball cap. Later, when they get the hang of it and want more of a challenge, you can try them on harder choices—a pair of slippers vs. a pair of slippers that looks like Barney and costs twice as much. Remember to make sure they understand that needs come first (even the Rolling Stones knew that getting what you need is more important than always getting what you want), but that wants are not bad. They're part of our budget, too.

What it teaches: At every level, from preschooler to teenager (frankly, at every level from preschooler to adult), it teaches you to be more sensitive to the difference between what you really need and what you want.

Starting to Work for Pay

What I'm going to say in this chapter may raise a few eyebrows: Your children should go on the family payroll. They should be getting an allowance *in the form of pay for work at specific jobs*—when they reach the age of three.

Not all parents will believe that their three-year-olds are prepared for this, so let me say a little bit about the philosophy before I get down to the details.

Kids are born with a sense of entitlement, which they absolutely need as infants. And they *are* entitled, as infants, to have all their needs met.

I'm certainly not trying to say that's changed drastically by the time your child reaches the age of three. But it will change before you know it, and I absolutely believe— and I've seen this prove out, time after time— that three is not too young to begin teaching life's important lessons. The groundwork is laid young.

One of life's most important lessons is this: The natural consequence of life is that money follows work. Remember "get it/spend it/save it/give it"? "Get it" has to come first. There are only two legal ways to get money—someone gives it to you out of the goodness of their heart, or you earn it. In the normal course of life, no one is going to give you enough to enable you to get by—and you probably wouldn't feel that good about yourself if you did live like that.

How do you know if your child is ready to earn it? Here's a simple test. If she can answer the question "What do Mommy and Daddy do with money in the store?" then she's ready.

After that, the more you go on just giving it to her, the more you're fostering entitlement. Don't be surprised if she learns that lesson and keeps expecting stuff.

But will she really understand the life consequence part?

Look at it this way. Kids are able to learn lots of life lessons when they're three years old—brushing their teeth, not talking to strangers, and stopping at red lights, for example. Do kids really understand why they have to do it—or even, at first, *that* they have to do it? Maybe not— they have to be reminded of each one of these rules a million times, and they may not understand the principles behind, say, long-term dental hygiene, but they can brush their teeth when they're told to, and if you keep telling them, gradually they absorb the lesson and the reason behind it.

We tend to feel differently about money. It's one thing to tell your three-year-old to brush his teeth—but isn't it much too early to burden him with the concept of financial responsibilities and obligations? Well, maybe it is. But just because your child isn't ready to understand the concept of traffic control, or exactly what a speeding car can do to her, would you hold off teaching her not to stop at a red light?

Your three-year-old *is* ready to understand what money does and *is* ready to start earning it. So how do you structure your child's earning the money, and—equally, if not more important—how do you structure his having it—spending, saving, and sharing?

Citizen of the Household

Work for pay means an allowance based on a specified series of chores that are *over and above* what is expected of your child, as part of either his personal development or his normal role as a contributing member of your household.

A child should never be paid for

> brushing his teeth . . .
> going to the potty . . .
> going to bed on time . . .
> crossing at the green . . .

or any other act that relates to personal hygiene or the development of personal responsibility and self-discipline.

He should also not be paid for what I call "Citizen of the Household" chores. These will vary from family to family, but the general rule is this:

Citizen of the Household chores are whatever everyone in the household is generally expected to chip in and do. In our household, citizenship chores for a three-year-old include these three:

> Put toys back in the toy box.
> Put clothes in the hamper.
> Help set and clear the table.

Work-for-pay chores are whatever you designate as a special chore that will become the child's special responsibility (for that week, anyway; chores can be changed or rotated between children if you have more than one). Our work-for-pay chores have included the following:

> Helping with dusting.
> Helping to sort recyclables.
> Organizing the flatware when emptying the dishwasher.

Notice that the jobs for three-year-olds are all "helping" jobs, *not* taking on full responsibility for a big job they're not ready to handle. You wouldn't ask a toddler to dust a whole room, but you can ask her to dust a coffee table while you're dusting the rest of the furniture.

Household Citizenship becomes much more of a topic later, when your kids are old enough to better understand the concept. We'll discuss it at greater length in the "School Age" section of this book, but right now it's an important part of life to start accustoming your children to. Citizenship and responsibility in the larger community all come out of the home.

How It Works

When your child turns three, she will start doing new chores around the house, and she'll be getting paid for working; the money will belong to her.

Start explaining all this to your child well in advance of her birthday, so it becomes an exciting rite of passage to being a big girl.

You shouldn't have any trouble with introducing this system—three-year-olds like to be helpful. And we're laying important groundwork again here—teaching the concept of money as part of a continuum. Spending doesn't exist in isolation from getting, getting doesn't exist in isolation from earning.

How much of an allowance do you give a three-year-old? I strongly recommend—in fact, this is one of the keys to making the whole program work—that as long as your child is on the work-for-pay allowance, you pay him his age. For a three-year-old, $3 a week, for a six-year-old, $6 a week, and for a twelve-year-old, $12 a week.

If you have a large family, or if your family finances are such that you absolutely can't afford that much, you can make it two-thirds or half—but stick to the same basic schedule, with a "raise" each birthday.

It really isn't as much as it sounds. The cost of living has gone up all around since you were little—for toddlers as well as grown-ups. And, as we'll see, this means only one dollar a week for your three-year-old to be actually spending. But it really is important to pay enough. If you pay a child too little, you're teaching her it's not worth it to work.

The Job Chart

Make up a list of chores that your preschooler can handle, and put a chore schedule someplace where you both can see it—the refrigerator is the most likely spot in most households. Here's a sample:

	Mon.	Tues.	Wed.	Thurs.	Fri.	Sat.	Sun.
Dust table							
Feed cats							

Explain to your child what all the chores on the chart are and how he'll be doing them, and you'll check them off with a big checkmark when he's completed them. Explain that at the end of the week, when all the boxes are checked in, he'll get his allowance of three dollars.

Use your judgment in making jobs—the chores shouldn't be so hard that you're slave driving your little preschooler (to put it another way, while they're so little, chores shouldn't become a chore), but they should be real—they should give him a real sense of helping.

A few other rules for chore making:

Rotate chores among your children. Chores should teach a variety of life skills equally to boy and girl children alike. Rotate even among children of different ages—although of course you'll prorate the amount of work. Where "dusting" for an older child may mean the whole living room, a little one will be expected to do only a single table.

The household rule for chores is "No work, no pay." This is one of the household values they should understand from an early age—but you're not really going to let a younger child sink or swim. It's all positive reinforcement. You'll remind him every day—"Now it's time to do our chores!"—and when he's finished, make a big to-do out of going right to his job chart and putting a big checkmark next to the chore. (Any ritual like this, involving words, is also a good area for reinforcement in teaching him his letters.)

At the same time, you'll also explain two other very important concepts to your child: the three jars and the good citizen chart, which goes on the refrigerator right next to the job chart.

The Three Jars

From the very first allowance your three-year-old receives, you'll be teaching him his first saving lessons. He's earned the money—now how does he budget it?

Pay your child her allowance in units of change—coins and bills—so the total can be divided into thirds (another counting game). Each third, you'll explain to her, goes into a different jar.

The first jar is quick change. This is the jar that she can take money out of at any time to spend on whatever she wants. When it's gone, it's gone, and there won't be any more until the next week.

The rules here are that you can't criticize what she spends her own money on. It's hers, and she earned it. You can have family rules, of course. If you don't allow toy guns in the house, or your child has a sugar allergy and can't be allowed sweets, she has to shop within those boundaries. But beyond that she's on her own.

This is an absolute hands-off rule, and it's one of the hardest for a parent to adhere to, and it's one of the most important. It is the bedrock foundation of teaching your child the first lesson of empowerment, self-confidence, and responsibility for her own choices. If she wants to spend her hard-earned dollar on a worthless piece of junk, you have to let her. If it breaks five minutes after she's bought it . . . well, it's not the last dollar she'll ever make.

She's been playing, and will continue to play, all sorts of store games and shopping games that will reinforce for her the awareness that you can buy different things for the same dollar. Making a foolish purchase with a dollar of her own will reinforce it even more strongly. You're undermining the whole process if you step in and prevent her from making her own mistakes—and you're undermining it just as much if you step in and buy her something new after her junky toy breaks.

The second jar is medium-term savings. This is the jar in which your child saves money for a larger purchase that he can buy for his weekly allowance.

This is a real learning process for your preschooler. Saving is not going to be a natural instinct for him. Deferred gratification is not one of life's pleasures that he'll arrive at without guidance. But it remains one of the most important life skills—a cornerstone for character building that's necessary to any teaching of values.

The medium-term savings jar is dedicated to buying something that your child really wants and that is within his ability—in terms of earning power and willpower—to save for and wait for.

In the case of a three-year-old, entering the glorious experiment of his first long-term savings venture, this means a very short exercise in deferred gratification.

Two weeks is about right.

Here, you'll need to give some guidance to your toddler. Go to the store with her, and talk about what you can buy if you save for two weeks. How much money will you have? What can you buy for two dollars? You'll have to make sure she understands that she can't buy the five-foot stuffed Barney for $40. But she can buy the Barney sticker book.

Together, pick out something that represents a realistic goal. If you can, put a picture of it on the jar to remind your child what it is she's saving for. Bring her back to the store some time in the middle of the week to show her the prize she's saving for—to keep her interest up, maybe even to help remember what she's doing. As soon as she's saved and bought a couple of things, she'll be much more involved. In about a year your child should be a skilled saver and able to defer gratification for four or five weeks or more.

The third jar is the long-term savings jar. Yes, your three-year-old is starting to save for college. Premature? No—habit building again. She won't exactly get the big picture here, of course, but then does she "get" oral hygiene?

When you get right down to it, most of us don't "get" saving as much as we ought to—Americans have the lowest rate of savings of any industrialized nation. Saving has to become a habit, like taking a multivitamin pill. In fact, sometimes making sure your kids start saving as three-year-olds, and keeping them at it, can have unexpected side benefits. I can't tell you how many parents have come up and told me, "I drilled saving into my kids long enough that finally it started to rub off on me."

The Good Citizen Chart

The reward for work is pay, the reward for behavior (being a good citizen) is a behavior-oriented treat.

Next to the job chart, keep a Good Citizen Chart (and call it that—the concept of good citizenship should start at home). On that chart, put your child's Citizen of the Household chart and award gold stars. An accumulation of gold stars isn't redeemable in cash, but maybe by means of a picnic or a family outing to the zoo or some other special place. Or you can set up a "treasure chest" —a grab bag of little toys in gift wrapping that your child can dip into after accumulating a certain number of gold stars.

Here's a sample gold star chart. You can cut a picture out of a magazine (or draw one yourself) to illustrate the treat at the bottom. As with the chore chart, you'll have the child check off the activity after she's done it, and then you stick on the gold star after you've verified it. Make sure you give plenty of praise along with the star—reinforcement should be verbal as well as visual!

	Mon.	Tues.	Wed.	Thurs.	Fri.	Sat.	Sun.
Brush teeth — morning							
Brush teeth —night							
Pick up toys							
Make bed							
Clothes in hamper							
Set table							
Clear Table							
Sunday Treat for All Gold Stars . . . Trip to the Zoo!!!!!							

Your Preschooler
and Values

A recent study by the Carnegie Task Force for Early Child Care reaffirms that infants need predictability, continuity, and the assurance that they're safe. Aren't these the same qualities that we all want to work for in our financial lives?

In fact, since our attitudes toward money are so personal, they probably do come, to some degree, from our earliest experiences. Psychologists have drawn lots of parallels between early infant experience and attitudes toward money—for example, rigid potty training and closeness with a dollar in adult life.

That's a little outside of the scope of this book, but I do want to emphasize that since little children's awareness is of the concrete, this is the age to focus on and reinforce the habits of personal hygiene and safety we've been talking about. They won't get the principle behind the action at first, and they don't have to. They just have to do it.

You'll have to remind very little children over and over again about these things, but that's the nature of habit building. You will have to budget your own time to allow for the reminders, to allow for stubbornness and distraction, so that these things will not only get done, they'll get done in the proper way—that is, with the child doing them herself.

And as much as you can, talk—in language your preschooler will understand—about why these things are important. Repetition is good. Enough repetition eventually internalizes a habit. Connecting the repetition of action to thought about the concept behind the action is even better; that is what leads to an understanding of values.

By "as much as you can," I mean two things. When you're dealing with issues of safety, immediate action always takes precedence. In certain instances the correct response is, *"WAAAAAAAAAAAAAAAAAAAAAA-AUUUGGGGGHHHHHH! Don't touch that Drano!"* accompanied by a flying sprint across the room. A reasoned explanation of safety is decidedly secondary.

When you're dealing with something you have to repeat a million times, like picking up toys, if you include the philosophy behind it every time, it can start turning into empty words. But don't forget that there are reasons for these rules, and articulating them increases by a whole lot the likelihood that your child will understand them.

Basically, values are learned at home. If your child has a consistent pattern of appropriate behavior, and he sees family rules and standards at work, he'll be getting the best possible lesson in proper behavior.

The Good Citizen Chart is a good tool in reinforcing these habits. As your preschooler gets older and is expected to take on more responsibility, you'll develop this into a system of rewards and punishments. For the little ones, you're trying to develop a win-win situation. You want to stress the idea that this is what we do, much more than this is what will happen to you if you don't.

Still, there may well be punishment situations sometimes.

Here's what I did when Kyle and Rhett were toddlers:

I didn't punish for not taking initiative (you can't expect that of little ones); I only punished for digging-in-the-heels recalcitrance: "No, I won't pick up the train set, and you can't make me."

Rewards for work are pay, rewards for good behavior are behavioral. Ultimately the punishment for not doing something is to do it. The key lesson here is the time value of time, and this is true even for little ones.

I made my preschoolers take "time out"—go stand in the corner and think about what they'd done. (I don't believe, in general, in sending children to their room. I think it's better if a room is a place of sanctuary, not punishment.) I made them stand there for five minutes. They could monitor the time themselves on the "time-out clock"—a clock with big numbers they could see from the corner. I would tell them that "when the big hand moves from the eight to the nine [or whatever], that will be five minutes, and you can come out. But then you have to tell me what you did that made Mommy send you to the corner."

This gave them a small but valuable lesson in the time value of time—the time in the corner meant that they couldn't be doing other things they would have preferred. (It also gave them a lesson in telling time, but I *don't* recommend this as your primary teaching technique.)

It also established communication between us, so that we were sure we both had the same understanding of what they were being punished for.

This is important. Very often you and your child may have a totally different concept of what has just happened. You do need to make sure he understands what you're doing and why you're doing it.

Don't make "time out" longer than your child's attention span, one minute per year, can handle. The idea is to make him think about what he has done and to feel the shame and embarrassment of being sent to the corner, not to give him a new play space.

If you have two children who are fighting, "time out" is a way of defusing the situation and giving them both time to cool off. Send them to separate places.

Remember, punishment is for bad behavior, not for being a bad person. It is supposed to be a learning experience.

In the section on school age kids, I'll talk about monetary "damages" for a transgression that costs someone else. It's premature to ask little ones to pay for things that are way beyond their tiny budget. Still, if your child breaks a playmate's toy, the situation needs to be dealt with.

Sometimes there's nothing that can be done. Very little children don't always have a strong concept of truth, and if you weren't there, you may never get to the bottom of what actually happened or who really broke the toy.

But if you're sure your child is responsible, your mission here is to connect behavior and consequences in your child's mind. That means two things:

First, act right away.

Second, explain in the simplest possible terms to your child what has to be done: "You broke Johnny's toy, and we have to get him a new one. We'll use your allowance to pay for part of it, and Mommy will pay for the rest of it. We'll go out and shop for Johnny's new toy tomorrow, and you can pay for your share out of your quick cash."

Make sure you tell her (remember, it's important to articulate *everything*): "Think about this the next time you're playing in someone else's house. You have to have respect for other people's things."

Make sure as well that you explain the point to the other child's parents, so that they don't undermine your position by trying to smooth over the situation, telling your child that it doesn't matter.

Responsibility

Good habits start with taking care of two different categories of responsibility—for self (safety, personal health and hygiene) and for others (Citizen of the Household).

Safety and personal hygiene habits include brushing teeth, eating healthy foods, getting ready for bath, proper toilet habits, learning to tie shoes, stopping at a red light, always using the car seat or seat belt when you go for a drive.

This last one is a good example of the value of talking about good habits. You don't expect a three-year-old to put himself into a car seat, but you'll know you're doing your job if a nanny or an aunt or uncle says, "Oh, it's only to the store—just hop in the front next to me," and your preschooler says, "No, we *always* use a car seat."

Safety habits also include some "don'ts," like not getting into the medicine cabinet or the cleaning supply closet, not running down the stairs, not running off in a crowd or a store, or not talking to strangers.

Citizen of the Household habits include picking up toys, putting clothes away, putting dirty clothes in the hamper, putting used tissues in the wastebasket, and whatever else you think is important—for example, helping Daddy or Mommy set the table for supper. They also include things like not throwing your food around at the table.

Here's a hint on picking up toys: Organization does not come naturally. If you set up a place for everything, in toy boxes, on shelves, in drawers, you'll give your child a framework to function in. If you label the shelves and drawers with words and pictures, you'll be helping your child with her prereading skills.

Again, I can't emphasize too strongly—make sure that plenty of cleanup time is budgeted into every playtime session (this is good discipline for you as well as for your child).

Don't forget that you want your children to understand that actions have consequences, and that punishment is for bad behavior, but you also want to strike a balance. Punishment should be fair, not too severe.

For example, what do you do when kids leave their toys lying around the family room? Your temptation is to say, "I'm taking them away from you," but in reality that's a little harsh, especially for expensive toys. Here's a solution my friend Tyler Black came up with: the Saturday Box.

The Saturday Box is the repository for toys that have been confiscated for being left around. But they're not confiscated forever; they're confis- cated until the next Saturday. That's long enough for a child to get the message.

Don't forget that Citizen of the Household habits are just part of citizenship. Proper deportment and good manners in public—in the store, in synagogue or mosque or church, on the street—are an extension of your child's citizenship responsibilities.

This may be as good a time as any to mention the obvious—that with all the goodwill and good parenting in the world, you can't—and shouldn't—expect things to go smoothly all the time. For example . . .

There was the time my sister Alison and I led joint family vacation expeditions to Walt Disney World. Rhett was five years old, and so was Alison's son Trevor. We were in one of the gift shops when things started to unravel.

Rhett spotted a bin full of Mickey Mouse ears and yelled across the store to Trevor (the first breach of manners), *"Hey, Trevor, how'd you like one of these?"* Compounding his lapse of citizenship, he sailed the beanie across the store to Trevor, who backed up to catch it and upset a whole display rack, sending it crashing around him as he fell and was momentarily lost from sight.

Alison, her heart in her mouth, flew across the store to save her poor, crushed, perhaps battered and bleeding child, only to find him lolling on top of the wreckage, proudly wearing the Mickey Mouse ears and saying, "Look, Mom, they fit! Can I buy them?"

Alison did what any red-blooded American mom would have done under the circumstances.

She lost it.

By the time I got to her side, she was saying things that I could not responsibly recommend any parent say to her child (but I can certainly understand how they might get said).

I said the first thing that came to mind: "Now, now . . . what would Donna Reed do in this situation?"

Well, it worked. It broke the mood of temporary and justifiable insanity and calmed Alison down.

At that point we should have straightened up as best we could and left quietly. But something impelled us to buy the Mickey Mouse ears after all. However, when Alison presented her credit card to the nineteen-year-old salesclerk, she was told: "This isn't your card."

"What do you mean, it isn't my card?" Alison asked, confused. "Do you want to see some ID?"

"No, I don't want to see any of your fake ID. I heard that other woman say your name. It's Donna Reed, and that's not the name on this card."

Everyone in the store who heard this and was over thirty collapsed in laughter.

Sharing

Absolutely crucial to the relationship between financial responsibility and life values is teaching the lesson that sharing is every bit as important as the others in the earn/spend/save/share formula. Don't expect your little ones to internalize the concept of sharing right away. Not only is it a learned life skill rather than an instinctive one, it also conflicts with other life skills your child may be developing at the same time, like territoriality as part of a sense of self. Still, it's important that you begin to teach the habit of sharing early.

The best techniques for teaching the concept of sharing are example, praise, and reinforcement. Example and praise are pretty self-explanatory. Be generous yourself—share what you have and talk about how good it makes others feel and about how good it makes you feel.

Reinforcement means you keep doing it and keep talking about it and explain "that's what nice people do."

Don't expect to get the message across right away, and don't expect that all your attempts to reinforce it are going to work. In the first place, saying that it's what nice people do and that it makes you feel good to do it, doesn't guarantee that it *will* make your toddler feel good to do it. Maybe after a while, with plenty of reinforcement—but not right away.

Also, don't expect the rest of the world to fall right in line and cooperate with your lessons. Once when Kyle was in preschool and I was the parent helper that day, I tried to convince her to share her tea set with a little boy in the class. The two of them were off together on one side of the room (don't try to teach sharing lessons in a crowd), and I talked to Kyle about how good it would make her feel to share. I could tell that she wasn't buying it completely, but she was at least willing to entertain the possibility. She divided the tea set into two equal parts and passed one pile over to the little boy. I told her what a good girl she was and asked her didn't it make her feel good; and as she turned around to answer me, he wound up with the plastic teapot and hit her in the head with it as hard as he could.

It is the moments when the lesson of sharing does start to get through that bring tears of joy to a parent's eyes. Here's one from Jennifer Rockefeller Nolan, who shared with us many wonderful insights about her own childhood in a family dedicated to social responsibility. She took her three-year-old son, Hunter, to McDonald's one day. He bought a package of two McDonaldland cookies, and on his way out he saw another little boy in the parking lot, crying. "I'm going to give him one of my cookies," Hunter said. "That'll cheer him up."

Jennifer's first response was to tell him, "You can't do that, it will just embarrass him, you can't get involved." The Rockefellers were always taught that part of the responsibility of wealth was not to insult the dignity of others by grandstand gestures of help where help hadn't been requested. But she stopped herself before the words formed. She knew that Hunter wasn't acting as a Rockefeller—he didn't have any consciousness of what being a Rockefeller meant. He was acting as a goodhearted, generous three-year-old just learning the joys of sharing.

Hunter went over and offered his cookie to the little boy, who took it and stopped crying.

These lessons do work, even if you're not sure that what you're saying has any effect. I found this out for myself when Rhett was barely five.

After getting his work-for-pay allowance, he took his quick cash down to the local grocery store to buy some candy. This was in New York City, and there was an old lady—probably homeless—in the line in front of him. She was fifteen cents short of being able to buy her groceries, and the man behind the counter was telling her that she'd have to put something back, when Rhett stepped up and told the counterman he would pay the extra fifteen cents.

At first everyone was nonplussed and more than a little embarrassed. The counterman, Rhett's caregiver, even the old woman herself told him no, don't be ridiculous, they couldn't take money from a baby.

But Rhett held his ground. "I know what I'm doing," he said. "This is the way it is—you help out people when they need it, and when you need it, people will help you out. That's how it works."

When people still weren't sure how to react, Rhett delivered the clincher: "I work hard for my money," he said, "and I have a right to do what I want with it. And I want to share it, because it's the right thing to do."

When he got home and I heard this story, Rhett was a little embarrassed when I cried and hugged him. "What's the big deal?" he wanted to know. "I didn't do anything special. You share with people who need it—that's the way it works."

Finally, about the limits of sharing:

It's okay—and important—for your child to have a special place that's for her alone and some special things that she doesn't have to share. This teaches its own lessons about respect for oneself, and for others as well. Your child must also recognize that other people are allowed to have special places. In fact, if you help her find her own special place and talk about how from now on this will be just for her, you're showing her that you respect her, and that you'll honor her privacy.

At the same time, you can continue to stress that privacy and sharing can coexist. If you have more than one child, and they share a bedroom or a playroom, it's a good idea to have a community toy box, so that in addition to "my space" and "her space," there's always "our space." And from time to time, buy a family toy that's expressly for sharing—a ball, flashcards, a video.

Don't insist on a young child sharing all the time. It's not realistic. Remember when we talked about fixed vs. variable expenses? Well, sometimes that can apply to behavior, too. You have to decide what rules you will absolutely never bend on and which ones you're going to ease up on a period of time, even though the rule is valid. Sharing *is* important, but there are some ages where territoriality is incredibly important to children, and you just have to roll with the punches and keep making your points as best you can.

Charity

Like sharing, charity is not the first concept your little children are going to grasp, and it's not one that you'll work on a lot with preschoolers. The work you do on sharing is laying the groundwork for it.

But there are charitable activities in which you can involve your preschooler. They can—with your help and encouragement—donate toys to Toys for Tots or other toy drives. They can donate clothes to a children's hospital. For the most part they're too young to understand very much about the concept of giving money to charity, but they can trick or treat for UNICEF.

Your example is important. Where appropriate, take your preschooler with you when you do volunteer work. Talk to him about what you're doing, and why it's important, and how it makes you feel. Talk about how we're lucky enough to have things—our health and family, as well as material comforts—and we can express our appreciation for our own good fortune by sharing.

Make sure your children know what all this means—that homeless children, for example, literally do not have homes. That's why it's important to take your children with you whenever you can if you do volunteer work. They should see what the other side of life is like and what working to help is all about.

At the same time, it's important for them to know that the labels "rich" and "poor" are not value judgments. People with advantages in life are not better than people without (this also applies to the talking to strangers rule—there's no guarantee that the well-dressed stranger with the briefcase is safer than the lady in rags with a shopping cart), and everyone can help, everyone can share. I learned this vivid object lesson during my own volunteer work, teaching a group of ghetto kids about handling money and starting a business. They didn't have much, but they gave of what they had to charity. They were every bit as committed to helping those less fortunate as any well-to-do suburban kids.

Gifts to Your Preschooler

Work for pay doesn't mean your entire relationship with your child is flint-hearted capitalist to employee. Of course you can still give gifts to your children, above and beyond birthdays, Christmas, or Chanukah.

A few words of caution, though: you're trying to teach your children the proper place of money in a system of values. Don't make gifts a substitute for time spent with kids, and don't make gifts an automatic offering in exchange for time unavoidably spent away—you don't *have* to bring home a gift every time you go on a business trip.

Gifts aren't an obligation. They're just one way of saying "I care."

Honesty

Honesty is another learned value. You can't expect children to understand it unless you explain it to them.

We've talked about the change-making games as one lesson in honesty, especially in the difficult lesson that withholding the truth is just as dishonest as actively telling a lie—if you get more than the correct change back, and you don't correct the clerk's mistake, you're stealing.

Children also have to be told that you can't just take something out of a store without paying for it. They have to be told (and this is a separate lesson) that they can't just take something out of someone else's house without getting permission. If your child "borrows" something from his friend's house without telling anyone he's doing it, don't overreact. Don't assume he knew he was doing something wrong, and don't ask him why he did it. That's really irrelevant and pretty easy to figure out. He did it because he wanted to.

Your job is to make him responsible for his behavior. He has to be told that what he did was wrong, and he has to give the toy back. You can go with him, but he must be the one to actually give it back.

On the way back home, you can discuss with your child how he would feel if someone took one of his toys. Suggest some alternatives—for example, that maybe next time he and his friend could share—he could offer to loan one of his own toys in exchange for the one he wants to borrow. But if this happens, you'll have to monitor it to make sure the toys are returned. Little children have a very difficult time understanding the difference between giving and lending, so these kinds of transactions have to be monitored carefully.

Value Beyond Money

We've discussed how important it is that your children begin to understand the value of money and the importance of absolute fairness in financial transactions.

It's equally important that they learn money isn't the only measure of value.

Make sure that you talk to your preschooler about values that go beyond money. For example, take a favorite book like *Goodnight Moon* or *The Velveteen Rabbit*—talk about how many times the two of you have read it and perhaps how your mother and father read it to you when you were little.

Something that "belonged to Grandma" may be worth far more to you and your family than its sale price when it was new or its resale value. It's part of the story of your family; it's part of your child's story of who she is and where she came from. Nancy Willard, an outstanding poet and award-winning children's book author, describes a tradition in her family: every Christmas the children would each get, as one of the presents, something "from the ancestors"—some little thing that had been in the family for a long time. It wasn't the most expensive Christmas present, but it was the one they valued most.

Part Two
School Age

Introduction

When your child enters school, she has irrevocably entered the real world.

She'll still be supervised and protected in many ways by you and by her teachers. There will still be games and lessons you can employ, fun and safe ways to learn about the value of money and the increasing intricacies of fair exchange.

But starting with kindergarten, and accelerating through the school years, your preschooler will be making more and more real-life decisions, and real-life transactions, involving the value of money and the development of values.

According to marketing expert Dr. James U. McNeal of Texas A&M University, children between the ages of four and twelve will spend approximately $1 billion *of their own money* on back-to-school supplies alone.

Note the italics. That's just their own discretionary income and just on their back-to-school stuff.

Actually, I just gave you that figure to break the news to you gently. According to Dr. McNeal's survey, kids in this age group have well over $8 billion a year of their own money, of which they spend $6 billion and save the rest.* (This is, incidentally, way, way, way above the national average for saving, which is more like 4 percent—it's a good start and a habit that needs to be encouraged.)

School-age children are very much in the real world.

---

*McNeal, James U. *Kids as Customers: A Handbook of Marketing to Children,* Lexington Books, 1992, p. 15.

For Older Children:
A Review

If you have been using this book right along, the "School Age" section is a natural progression from what has come before. If you're starting this program with an older child, your first task is to determine what his financial skills are.

Here are some yardsticks:

Can she explain to you how a credit card works? (Should be proficient by age seven to nine.)

Can you send him to the grocery store with money and a shopping list? Can he buy all the items on the list and calculate the correct change? (Should be proficient by age eight to ten.)

At a restaurant, can she total the bill, compute the tax, and figure out how to leave a 15 percent tip? (Should be proficient by age eight to ten.)

Can he explain to you what interest is and how it works? (Should be proficient by age nine to eleven.)

Can he write out a check stub and balance the checkbook? (Should be proficient by age eleven to thirteen.)

Use these guidelines to figure out your child's current level of financial expertise. Then, even if she's older, your first step should be to go back and use or adapt whatever exercises and games she needs to get up to speed.

If your older child—even up to the beginning of high school—needs a graphic illustration of how basic financial processes work, I recommend starting him out with the jar system. This is also a good idea for any child who has not learned habits of financial responsibility, because it shows so vividly the process, and the benefits, of deferred gratification. How you do this will depend on the age of your child and how much she has to learn. You don't want to humiliate her with exercises that are too babyish, but you do want to make sure she understands basic concepts.

Expanding the Jar System

The three jar system I described in the preschool section is good for giving your kids the experience of deferred gratification (with the medium-term savings jar) and good for getting them involved in thinking about their future. The one dollar a week that your three-year-old puts aside may not go very far toward defraying the cost of a college education . . . but it doesn't hurt, either. And it teaches her, very early along, not only the habit of saving, but a real consciousness that she owns her own future—both literally and figuratively.

With school-age kids, however, there are more lessons to be learned from their allowance, so the jar system becomes more elaborate. It's still based on the three jars, and they still have the same function: quick cash, medium-term savings, long-term savings. But now the three-way division is based on *net earnings,* not gross.

Use those terms in explaining the new jar structure to your child. Understanding what they mean is another life skill. Just as the lawn service person doesn't end up with the whole $25 an hour in his pocket, your child has to understand early that living in society, and functioning in society, has its price. And paying that price is part of being a good citizen.

Your school-ager is going to start paying taxes.

If you've been following these ideas from the time your toddler first started playing his "going to the store" games, you've been telling him about taxes right along. If you're starting out a school-age child on the system, you'll need to start explaining them now. You'll have to start making him understand that taxes are not only what people gripe about and make jokes about, they're a part of the fabric of our society.

Your school-ager is a Citizen of the Household, and he's in the 15 percent tax bracket: 15 percent of his weekly allowance goes into the tax jar. (It's good practice to learn to calculate 15 percent in any case. It's a figure he'll use in other areas of life, like tipping.)

His taxes go into the family fund we describe in the family banking chapter on page 92. This is, in other words, a lesson in representative democracy.

When I went to grade school, we studied about the Founding Fathers and the American Revolution, and one of the phrases that was pounded into us until we knew it by heart was "No taxation without representation." We knew it by heart, but we didn't know what it meant.

But in your family banking pool, you have taxation *with* representation. The money goes for the benefit of the whole family, and the whole family discusses and votes on what it gets used for.

Taking a withholding tax out of your child's paycheck, and explaining why you're doing it, can go a long way toward helping to bypass a syndrome that can come up a few years down the road, which I call "paycheck shock." They say that in this life you can count only on death and taxes, and since you only die once, taxes are a much more frequent certainty. But no one tells you how often it's going to happen to you—not once a year on April 15, but every time you get a paycheck.

Paycheck shock, if no one warns you, hits with the first paycheck you get on your first real job, when that $220 a week that you thought you'd be making turns into $163.32. At my own first payday, as a sixteen-year-old working at Bloomingdale's in New Jersey, I stormed into my boss's office, demanding, "Who's this FICA person, and why are you paying him out of my paycheck?" We all too commonly make up our budget by figuring in pretax dollars, then wonder why we can't live up to it with our after-tax dollars.

Second, your school-ager is going to participate as a citizen of the larger community, too. Another 10 percent of his allowance goes into a charity jar.

The sooner your child gets used to the idea of charitable giving as an integral part of her financial life, the better. Giving is a learned, not a natural, response. It has to be learned. If it's initiated this early in your child's life, you have a good chance to make it a habit, a natural part of what your child does with her money.

The remaining 75 percent, your child's net allowance, goes into the other three jars.

This is part of what happens with money in the real world, but it's not the whole story. Money that's saved or invested earns interest, and that's another valuable lesson you can teach your kids. Deferred gratification can be worth tangible rewards; good habits can pay you back.

The natural consequence of saving is that it earns you money.

Conversely, the natural consequence of borrowing is that it costs you money.

So I recommend that you give your kids interest on their savings. Give them a smaller rate of interest on the money in their medium-term savings jars and a higher rate on the money in their long-term jars. Quick change, like the money we all carry in our pockets, earns no interest.

Actually, since you're dealing with relatively small sums of money and relatively short amounts of time, if you calculated interest on the same basis that a bank does, the figures would be so small as to be meaningless.

So while it's important to teach your children how real interest rates work (I'll go into this, with charts, in the "Family Banking" chapter, page 92), it's best to use a vastly simplified version for your children's jars—something like this:

For savings of $1–$10, medium-term savings:	7¢ per week
For savings of $1–$10, long-term savings:	12¢ per week
For savings of $10–$20, medium-term savings:	17¢ per week
For savings of $10–$20, long-term savings:	23¢ per week

This means that you'll need a lot of change, including pennies, to disburse every week, and it can get to seem like a lot of bother. I recommend keeping a change jar or dish. Empty your pockets into it in the evening, and you'll always have change for all these little coin obligations.

Two other notes on this subject. First, this creates an opportunity for a very nice gift your kids can make for you—a decorated change jar. Second, a stitch in time saves nine—bothering with these details now, when your children are young and learning their lifetime habits, will pay off in the long run.

Your kids can't forget, either, that part of their income will be used for gifts; they'll have to take holiday budgeting into account and set up a Christmas club (we'll describe all this in detail in the "Giving and Receiving" chapter on page 136).

If your kids are learning about computers, this whole system is a great exercise for those skills. They can computerize the whole expanded jar system, including a calendar for date planning (how many weeks till Christmas? how much saved in the Christmas club?), pie charts for dividing up money and figuring interest and taxes, charts for computing how much they've saved toward a long-term goal, how much they still have to save.

Educational Resources has an extensive catalog of educational software for kids, which they sell to schools and homes. Call to receive their catalog: 1-800-624-2926.

Family Meetings

Your school-age child, even your five-year-old kindergartner, is old enough to be a full-fledged participant in your family meetings. These are the meetings where goals and plans are made, where rules are discussed, and—very important in a household where the value of money is a key tool in the teaching of values to your children—where budgets and budgeting are discussed.

It's important before getting into a detailed discussion of what a family meeting is, to point out what it is not. It's not a legislative body. A household is not and cannot be a democracy, though it can and should encourage participation, and respect the opinions of, all members of the family. Ultimately, though, it is the parents who make the decisions—unless it's been specifically decided, before a discussion starts, that it will be put to a binding vote.

This is, after all, the way the real world works, too. Work on a job isn't democratic either. With luck, you can be in an organization where employee input is encouraged, or have a boss who'll solicit your opinions, but ultimately a business organization, whether it be a large corporation, small retail store, or college faculty, is hierarchical.

This is an important distinction, and one that kids should understand early. All parents have heard gripes from their kids ranging from "I thought we were supposed to be living in a democracy" to "Didn't Lincoln free the slaves?" Explaining the difference between democratic and hierarchical structures, in addition to being a valuable lesson in citizenship, will head off many of those complaints. In much the same way, explaining the difference between work for pay and Citizen of the Household chores will head off another situation that can arise all too easily: kids demanding to be paid for everything.

The family meeting can, however, teach a wide variety of life skills to your kids: decision making, goal setting, problem solving, negotiating, brainstorming, arbitration, creative thinking in a group, and public speaking, to name a few. It can be a situation where children learn to show respect for the ideas of others and learn also that their ideas can be respected.

Problem solving in a group is a particular and important life skill. This is a good place for your child to start learning the art of listening—another one of those talents that doesn't come naturally. Here's a good art-of-listening exercise for family meetings—when someone is responding to a point that someone else has made, have her restate the original point in her own words before going on to the response.

Family meetings should be held on a set schedule, in a special place that feels at least a little ceremonial. The dining room is good if you have one; the kitchen table is just fine, too. You can make it look a little more official with little notepads and pencils at every seat or just a sign announcing the family meeting.

Once a month is a good interval for a family meeting, although you may choose to have them more frequently, like once every two weeks. Pick a day and a time when everyone is likely to be at home and when the little ones aren't too tired.

You should also have some provision for emergency family meetings, if something comes up that absolutely has to be discussed. By the way, if the emergency meeting concerns a family member (for example, someone not doing his chores), that family member has to be there—he can't be excluded.

Your preschoolers should be encouraged to sit in on family meetings, but you have to understand that they will not be able to focus on everything that's going on, and they may want to color or will wander off and play with toys. This is all right—but by the time they're of school age, they should start being active participants.

Once again, as with all these rites of passage, make sure your child is given ample preparation for this new right and responsibility: "When you start school, then you'll start coming to the family meetings and sitting right at the table with Mommy and Daddy and the bigger kids"—or whatever your family structure is.

A family meeting begins with a *written agenda,* and all the decisions that are made for the family should be recorded in a *family journal,* which becomes a permanent record for your family.

The journal should be kept where everyone can have access to it—in the family room, in a special drawer in the kitchen, or on the family computer.

Everyone should be encouraged to submit items for the agenda to the family member who's the group leader for the upcoming meeting. This doesn't have to be any sort of formal submission.

Everyone in the family takes turns being group leader, and everyone takes turns being recording secretary. Use your judgment on this: your five-year-old probably isn't ready for either job, but your eight-year-old may be. Most kids should be able to start taking on the responsibility at somewhere between eight and ten.

It doesn't matter how big or small your family is: if you're a single parent or guardian with one child, you deserve the same respect as a family unit, and it's every bit as important for you to treat family functions with the respect and ceremony they deserve. If you and your child are swapping turns, at each meeting, at being recording secretary and group leader, that's fine, too.

There are ways you can help the younger ones think in terms of contributions to the family agenda—ways that will also continue to encourage them to think in terms of value. The product test report is an excellent tool for this.

The Product Test Report

Choose a product that the family uses and that the child knows about. The idea here is that she can be as much of an expert, as knowledgeable an authority on this product, as anyone else in the house. Breakfast cereal is an excellent product to start on (this is also the smart consumer game, which we'll be talking about later).

Tell the child that she can organize a family discussion on what kind of cereal the family should be eating. She has to investigate all the qualities that go into making a desirable cereal. What are they? Pictures of favorite cartoon characters on the box? Maybe not. What about nutrition? Price? Taste?

She can select products from TV commercials, from newspaper or magazine ads, mail-order coupons, or any other source (one of the goals of her research can be to prove or disprove the advertising claims). She can begin her research in the store, by reading labels and comparing prices. Then she can bring her preliminary findings back to the family meeting, present them, and apply to the family for a budget to continue her research. She'll have to explain how many cereals she needs to taste-test and why.

A tip here: The first time your child makes a presentation like this, it is going to be almost unbearably cute and endearing. Try to appreciate this aspect of it quietly and internally—save your reaction for the phone call to Grandma the next day. For her, it's going to be serious stuff. She'll have worked hard on this presentation, and she'll want to be taken seriously.

Anyway, she'll apply for a *family grant* to continue her research, and the family can discuss it. She'll make her case, and then the family can vote to approve or disapprove (well, you won't do that) or approve with reservations. You don't have to approve the whole grant. You can authorize her to buy five boxes of cereal instead of the seven she's asked for. Of course, if she wants to go over budget, she can use her own quick cash.

Then, at the next family meeting, she'll present the results. First she'll give some background: compare the real value of the different products to their advertising claims. Then she'll make a case for the cereal she's chosen: it delivers more for the money, it doesn't get mushy in milk, it tastes so demonstrably better that it's worth the extra half cent a serving.

She can include other aspects of the product, too: What's the packaging like? Is it wasteful? Recyclable?

If two or three of them are equal, she can narrow it down to two finalists and present them to the family for a blindfold taste test.

The lessons learned here are determining relative value, research, some math, judging monetary value as part of a larger picture (the more expensive cereal may also be more nutritious), and presentation of a project to an audience.

Oh, one more thing on the cereal project: Suppose one of the incentives to buy a certain brand of cereal is a really cool prize. How should this figure in?

Well, like everything else, it shouldn't be dismissed out of hand. Let her calculate that as part of the total package. How much would the prize be worth if you bought it at a store? How much, if anything, does it add to the price of the cereal as compared to a similar cereal with no prize? This can be a good one, because of course if the family buys the cereal so she can get the prize for free, then she'd be asking the family to subsidize her toy buying, which is unfair.

The cereal product test report—or something like it—is a good way to introduce your children to participation in family meetings. Later on they can apply the same techniques to much more difficult research projects.

Consider these other items for family meetings that translate into solid value-oriented learning experiences:

Making Major Purchases

Ultimately you're not going to put buying a new car to a vote. But the kids can be included in a terrifically educational need vs. want discussion here. What do you actually need in a new car? How much passenger room? How much cargo room? What about safety factors? Gas mileage? Frequency of repairs?

What do you want? A CD player? Velour seat covers? A computerized trip planner? How much can the family afford to pay for extras, and what are the priorities? What should be the factors in prioritizing extras (for example, who uses the car most)?

You can put the kids in charge of figuring out these factors. Have them make a list of wants and needs in the family journal. Take them with you to the car dealer, and have them get prices for all the options you're considering.

There's an extra value here. This will also give your kids experience in listening to, and evaluating, a salesperson's pitch. A car salesperson is like a TV commercial in real life, and it's a totally different experience for a child. Explain to them that you don't debate with the salesperson, and you don't give her the response she's looking for, which is "I'll take it!" You take the information from the salesperson, you make notes, you go home and discuss it.

Make sure your kids understand that if TV commercials are calculated to persuade you, salespeople—with that in-person, human touch—are going to be even more persuasive. If your kids feel that they *want* to get caught up in the salesperson's enthusiasm, that's what they're supposed to get caught up in. It's perfectly normal—but they don't have to act on it.

Make sure, also, that your kids know that research should not be a never-ending project. Decide, in a family meeting, how many car deal-erships you're actually going to visit (three is a good number). Then visit that many—no more, no less—and compare the information you've gathered. Accept the fact that it's always possible you could have gotten a better deal (and after you've made the purchase, someone is sure to tell you about it). Your time is worth something, too—and endlessly chasing around after the perfect deal is a waste of your time.

After you've made the rounds of your three dealers—and decided on the make and model of the car you want—your kids can enter the prices of various options in the journal, and the family can discuss them in terms of the total budget for the car and the relative importance of each different option.

Let's take a couple of different cases.

Suppose your kids want an expensive stereo system for the car. You like music, too, but as long as the sound quality is clear enough so that you can make out the difference between "The Star-Spangled Banner" and "Blue Suede Shoes," you're happy.

Now, none of this is a need. But part of it (having a car stereo) is an agreed-upon want, and the other part (having a terrific car stereo) is an extra want. How much extra? Let them research it. Is it cheaper to get it as an option with the car or go to a car stereo dealer? Can you and/or your kids learn how to install it themselves and save money that way?

Now you have the figures. Do your kids want it enough to pay the dif-ference?

Second case: Your kids want fireball racing stripes painted on the side of the car. They've researched it, gotten a price for it, are willing to pay for it.

Only problem: This is a family car, and you won't be caught dead dri-ving it with fireball racing stripes.

The bottom line: You win. It doesn't matter if they'll pay for it; every-one has to live with it, so everyone has to accept it.

I speak here from experience. I want the family van to be painted with cow spots, and I'm willing to pay for it. I've even researched getting a car horn that will moo (yes, they make them). The only trouble: My kids will not even agree to live in a house that has a cow van parked in the drive-way. Of course, in this case we reached a fair and reasonable compro-mise: I'm doing it anyway.

What about debatable areas? For example, are four doors a need or a want? This is the sort of thing that depends on your family's usage pattern and can legitimately be debated in a family meeting.

But in the case of a major purchase, it must be made very clear, up front, that the children will have input and consideration, but they will not have a vote on the final decision.

Vacation Planning

Again, this is a marvelous research project, involving all sorts of reference books and trips to the library, the making of visual presentations (as elaborate as your kids want to make them, with visual displays, flip charts, graphs, and so on), and the preparing of budgets that will challenge your child's creativity as well as his math skills.

A vacation is another area where you'll be discussing the balance between the bottom line and value that can't be figured in dollars. Will there be educational benefits to one vacation spot over another? Should making sure you all see Grandpa be an important factor?

Should a family vacation be left up to a vote? You'll have to decide on this one. But if you're reserving the final decision for yourself (which is certainly acceptable—a vacation's no small expense), make sure that's very clear before you bring up the matter for discussion.

Gift Giving

Ceremonial gifts—a wedding, a graduation—may be from the whole family, so the whole family can discuss them. Such discussions can be good occasions for talking about the appropriateness of different kinds of gifts and the budgeting of different gifts for different people. These are concepts that can be difficult for younger children. Frankly, they can be difficult for anyone.

Charities

Built right into the whole concept of the family meeting is the celebration of the family: how lucky you are to have each other, to have a home and food on your table, to have the kind of family communication that enables you to meet like this and discuss issues of importance to all of you.

Recognizing that others are less fortunate, and doing something to help, is a key element in this celebration—I firmly believe, in fact, that the celebration is hollow without it.

If you have a charity of your own, your child is probably already familiar with it. If you've talked about it or, better yet, taken your child with you to do volunteer work for the charity, then that will probably become your family's charity. If not, and you're just beginning the practice of family meetings, this is a good time for the family to discuss a charity or charities.

Certainly any family can be involved in more than one. If your child becomes interested in a cause or an area of need, he can bring it up at a family meeting and present a case for it.

I suppose there would be a certain logic to saying, "Then the family can vote on it," and in theory I guess that's a good idea. In practice, if a child cares so passionately about a cause (unless, upon investigation, it turns out to be a rip-off), I can't imagine not finding a way to include it in the family charitable plan.

By the way, if it is a rip-off, it's almost certain to be the organization, not the societal need, that's suspect. A little more investigation by the family will very likely turn up another organization that speaks to the need your child has recognized.

Don't forget that when it comes to charitable giving, a commitment of time is just as important as a commitment of money, and it has to be scheduled in. In our family, we know we're going to trick or treat for UNICEF, and we have the date marked on the family calendar, so nothing else is planned for that date. And a few times every summer we come up to volunteer at Opus 40, the monumental environmental sculpture and fine arts organization located in Saugerties, New York.

Family Finances

How much should you talk about family finances in front of your children? How much should they know about the family's overall financial health?

Perhaps more than you think. If you argue at all about money (and most people do—at least sometimes), then there's a good chance your children have already experienced some discussion of family finances. So that's all the more reason to make sure that they hear more than just arguing—that they have the experience of listening to calm and reasoned discussions of the family budget.

It's not necessary for younger children to know every detail of your financial life, although they will gradually be included more and more, as they get older. But they should know, in general, how things are going—whether times are good or tight.

Gradually you will involve your children more and more in the family finances. These areas ought not to be secret—they have a right to know, and sometimes they have responsibility to know, the ups and downs of the family they're a part of.

By the time your children get to be eleven or twelve (once again, you're the best judge of your own children's level of maturity and responsibility), you're ready for the next phase of their involvement: the family bill-paying project.

Don't put it off until they get to be teenagers. It really is true that teenagers, if they're not disabused of this notion early, can start thinking that money grows on trees. A responsible eleven- or twelve-year-old, who still considers it a privilege to be given family responsibility, is the perfect candidate for this project.

The family bill-paying project is exactly what it sounds like: the family sits down and pays its bills together.

Set up a special ledger for this. It should have the following columns in it:

The total amount of money available for paying bills. If you want to, you can actually show your child your pay stub, so he can see that taxes, Social Security, and so on have been deducted from it. If you'd prefer not to do this, then make sure you let him know that a certain percentage of your total income gets deducted for taxes and what that percentage is.

A column in which all the bills are listed—mortgage or rent, utilities, credit cards, cable TV, car payment, and so forth.

A column next to each bill for "minimum payment due" and one for "total balance due."

A column in which monthly cash expense items—food, gasoline, car fare, entertainment, and so on—are listed.

A column in which the estimated dollar amounts for each item are listed.

A column in which medium-term savings items are listed.

A column for the dollar amounts for each item.

A column in which long-term savings items are listed.

A column for the dollar amounts for each of these items.

The ledger will look something like this:

Total $ available	Monthly Bill	Minimum payment	Full payment	Cash Expense	$ amount	Medium—term savings goal	$ amount
	Mortgage			Food		Tires for car	
	Fuel			Gasoline		School field trip	
	Electric			Carfare		Stereo	
	Car			School Supplies			
	Cable			Entertain-ment			
	American Express						
	Visa						
	Insurance						
	Total						

Have your child take all the bills and write down the amount owed next to each bill on the ledger. If both a "minimum payment due" and a "total balance due" are listed on the bill, he'll write both figures. For bills that have to be paid in full, he'll put the same amount in both columns.

Then have him total up both columns and compare them with the money on hand (the "Total $ Available") of the first column.

What's the difference between money on hand and total bills owed? If you pay everything, will there be enough left over for cash expenses and savings?

If there is enough to pay the full amount of each bill, the next part is simple. Together, you write the checks and put them in the envelopes.

If there isn't, then before you start writing checks, you have to decide which bills are going to be paid only in part. Explain to him about interest payments—that you will have to pay more money, in the long run, for making only partial payment on a bill.

Let him come up with a strategy for which bills to pay in full and which to pay in part. Discuss his reasons for his choices (ultimately you're the one who'll have to make the final decisions).

Discuss with your child whether there's any way to economize so that the monthly bills are lowered. This can be a good time to explain to him about fixed and variable expenses.

Sometimes parents tend to be afraid that their children shouldn't know that they're doing well; they worry that it will make the children greedy or snobbish. They worry that if the children know the family is doing well, they won't be able to hold out against arguments along the lines of "The Joneses next door have a built-in swimming pool; why shouldn't we?"

But there is a good two-pronged answer to that one. First, "our rules." Second, you're not telling your children only that you're doing well; you're sharing with them the whole picture of your family's budgeting and goal setting. Your kids must know that there will always be families with more than you have, and there will always be people with less—and that it's important to try to help those who have less, not envy those who have more. (Note—when you explain this to your children, I recommend using these words, not euphemisms like "less fortunate" and "more fortunate." It's true that good fortune, or good luck, came to be associated in our language with having a fortune or having lots of money. But you don't want to reinforce, for your kids, the idea that having or not having a lot of money is what makes you fortunate or unfortunate.)

If it's part of an overall program of financial responsibility, this should not become a problem that gets out of hand.

On the other hand, if things are tight and you need to cut back, your children need to know that, too. You don't want to scare them. Kids don't have a clear sense of proportion, especially when it comes to numbers that are outside their everyday experience, and they need to be reassured that "we'll be okay—you'll always have food and clothes and a roof over your head, and you'll always be loved, but right now we have to stay on a tighter budget than before."

You also shouldn't apologize for things being tight. You don't need to feel guilty about it. This is how life works. In the long run, being honest about it is a way of empowering your kids, giving them the strength to deal with change.

If the family has to stay on a tighter budget, what does that mean for the kids' allowance?

We've been through this; we've had tough times, as most families do. I've explained it to my kids and asked them if they would contribute part of their allowance to the general budget. They've always understood, and they've always agreed. It's been an empowering experience for them; it makes them aware that they're a part of the family.

My kids are young. Older kids, when things get tough, can do more, and if they have solid values, they'll not only want to do more, they may want to do more than they can: your fourteen- or fifteen-year-old may want to drop out of high school and go to work full-time to support the family.

Here again, the more honest you've been about family finances, the more you'll be able to strike a balance. This actually happened in my family: when I was sixteen, our comfortable middle-class existence was shattered when my father left home and left us penniless.

None of us, not even my mother, had been included in the family financial picture, and that made it much harder to adjust. We were all in the same boat, and we all had to learn together; this was my first lesson in family budgeting and family financial honesty. My sisters and I went to work and took the responsibility for college upon ourselves.

We didn't drop out of school: in our family, the importance of education was too strong, and we studied it out and understood that in the long run our dropping out would be a financial liability to the family.

What if you give the kids the option of contributing back some of their allowance, and they choose not to? Don't be judgmental; if you've given them a choice, you're making an implied contract that you'll accept whatever choice is made. You can, however, make sure they understand that the money has to come out of somewhere: a family movie or desserts.

In any case, whether you ask the kids to contribute back or tell them that it has to be that way, it is very important to make it clear that this is not a punishment—it's part of a family belt-tightening that everyone shares in.

Be careful, in general, of making vague and misleading statements about the nature of your family finances. "We can't afford it" is *not* an appropriate response when what you really mean is "I'm not going to buy that for you." "We can't afford it" can frighten kids, or it can make them suspect hypocrisy, if they can *see* money being spent . You can't assume that a child will know about budgeting, or know money is finite, or know that there's no such thing as a magic plastic card, unless you explain it to him.

Household Rules

Some household rules—like curfews—are nonnegotiable; others really can be determined by family discussion. Your own family needs and dynamics will dictate your household rules, but here are a few suggestions.

Telephone message-taking etiquette is important to everyone. If you run a business from your home, you can't have your kids answering the phone in an unbusinesslike way. If you're fifteen, you should be able to count on a family member not calling you to the phone with, "Hey, Shari, it's that creepy guy Dennis with the pimples who you said was such a nerd!" In either case, you should be able to count on actually getting all your phone messages.

I wrote out a phone scenario for Kyle and Rhett and posted it next to every phone extension in the house, along with the 911 and other emergency numbers (which every kid should know and be able to differentiate—that's another good project for family meetings). I also provided a pencil and a phone pad, which looked like this:

```
Date _____ Time _____
For _____
Caller _____
Message _____
_____
_____
```

Of course this system doesn't work as perfectly as it should unless the phone pad and pencil are in place at all times, so making sure of that can be a designated household chore.

My phone scenario goes like this:

> *"Children's Financial Network, may I help you?"*
>
> *(The caller asks for Neale Godfrey. If Neale Godfrey is at the store, or talking to the president of the United States on the other line, or in the bathroom, or chasing mice around the kitchen with a rake and a giant water balloon, the response is the same): "I'm sorry, she is unable to come to the phone right now. May I take a message?"*
>
> *(If the caller says "No, I'll call back," a simple "Good-bye" is fine here. If the caller wants to leave a message):*
>
> *Take the first and last name.*

Repeat the first and last name, ask caller to spell it out, write it down.

Take the message.

Repeat it all back, including the caller's name.

Thank the person for calling, tell them you'll give Ms. Godfrey the message, and say good-bye.

Here's a real-life situation that came up not long ago in one of our family meetings. Since I had given up my apartment in New York and moved my entire base of operations into my home in the suburbs, I needed more office space. My current arrangement, which was no office space at all, was beginning to become decidedly unsatisfactory. I decided to look into building a new wing on the house for an office and an enlarged kitchen.

That euphoria lasted until I got estimates on the job and discovered quickly that we are not new wing–type folks. If I was going to have an office, it was going to have to be in a space that already existed in the house.

We live in an old farm-style house that has a kitchen, a dining room, and a family room on the ground floor, two smallish rooms on the third floor, and three rooms on the second floor: my bedroom and two other rooms that are perfectly adaptable to office space.

Unfortunately those rooms were occupied at the moment by Kyle and Rhett.

There was a solution, and preliminary estimates indicated that this solution would cost about one-tenth what the new wing would have: remodel the third floor and make bedrooms for Kyle and Rhett up there. Put my office into the vacated second-floor bedroom.

I brought this up at a family meeting. The responses basically fell into two categories.

The first was: "No way!"

The second was: "It's not fair!"

But it was the only way it could work. I really did need the space for work; and because it was going to be a primary work space, I was going to be spending most of my time there.

So the kids couldn't have a say in whether it would happen, but they could have major input in how to make it happen, and this became the new focus of a lively and animated family meeting.

We agreed to set aside a budget for the remodeling job. Ceilings could be raised, dormers could be put in. Walls could be knocked down or put up. The kids could, working within a budget, create their own environment.

The picture started to change. The kids came to understand that the move had to be made, and better than that, they were involved in an exciting new project.

They had their own ideas, of course, about creating an environment, but they also understood that want vs. need issues came first. What needed to be done to make the third floor a habitable space? How much would it cost? The architect talked to them and offered them a series of problems and solutions.

As they continue planning, Kyle and Rhett are learning invaluable lessons about several important concepts:

How much things cost in the real world
How much things cost *relative to each other* in the real world
Long-term planning
Architecture and construction
Need vs. want

They'll be living with their decisions until they go away to college, so they're learning some important lessons about the consequences of decision making. And it's making them think long and hard. I'll be interested to see what they finally come up with.

Family Banking

You can use your family meetings to work out a system of group participation in finances, which I call "family banking." It's another excellent demonstration of how we can use money as a socializing force. The family bank can bring a family together to create and set the rules for projects you'll do together. It's another way of making people comfortable about the idea that money is a tool, and that the wise use of that tool can promote family and community health.

In essence: There should be a pool of family money, and the family should discuss how this is raised and how it's administered. The money can come from *taxes, gifts, family projects,* or *family saving strategies.*

The family, of course, should decide how to create the family money pool. Here's a chart worksheet we've found useful, along with a few sample ideas for filling it out. You can come up with ideas that work for you in your family meeting.

You can probably think of any number of money-saving ideas of your own to add to this list. There are also some good books out these days by people who have developed saving a nickel here and there to a science, or perhaps an art (like *The Tightwad Gazette,* by Amy Dacyczyn; Villard Press).

Another source of income that we use for the family money pool is the *penalty jar,* which we instituted to teach the kids how to pay attention to things that drive us crazy (and cost us money) when they don't pay attention to them.

The things that drive us crazy mostly have to do with leaving things on—leaving the TV on, the computer on, the lights on in a room that you've left. For other families, it may also include leaving things

Ways to Earn Money	What Needs to Be Done	Who'll Organize	Earning
Yard Sale	Gather stuff. Figure prices. Tag items. Set up. Take down.		
Bake Sale	Buy ingredients. Bake stuff. Figure prices. Tag items. Set up. Take down.		
Ways to Save Money	What Needs to Be Done	Who'll Organize	Saving
Make your own Xmas ornaments	Figure out how many ornaments you would normally buy each year, how much you would normally spend. Plan ideas for home-made ornaments (like stringing popcorn). Price out raw materials for home-made ornaments.		
Save gift wrapping	Gather up the wrapping paper and fold it. Find some place to store it. Remember where you stored it.		

Ways to Save Money	What Needs to Be Done	Who'll Organize	Saving
Save on energy bills	Research how much you'll save for each degree the thermostat is lowered. Decide how much temperature reduction you'll all be comfortable with (be considerate of someone who has to do sedentary work at home). "Sweater police."		
Save on energy bill — #2	Figure out how much it costs per minute to take a shower with hot water. Discuss how long the average shower in your household is; decide how much you can shorten it by.		
Food Coupons	Search the paper for coupons *for items the family uses regularly.* Clip and organize coupons.		

open, like the refrigerator door or an outside window when the heat is on. The key here is that driving you crazy isn't enough—these annoyances also have to cost money. This is the rule of natural consequences. The consequence of leaving the refrigerator door open is that it wastes money; the penalty for it should be monetary.

Everyone in the family has a penalty jar. At the beginning of the year we put $10 in quarters into each jar (this is a good counting exercise for a little one). Every time someone violates a penalty jar rule (you'll set these rules at your family meeting, and they'll be written down in the family journal so that everyone knows about them) it costs a quarter, and the quarter goes into the family bank. At the end of the year the kid gets to keep whatever is left in the jar. Of course, as with all other income, this gets divided among the jars.

There's one more wrinkle to the penalty jar stratagem and one more lesson to be learned. If I walk into the TV room, and MTV is blaring Snoop Doggy Dogg to an empty room (not a bad idea, actually, but this isn't a book of music criticism), I'll ask who did it. With any luck, the kid who did will own up. The fine is a quarter from the penalty jar, and that money goes into the family pool. If no one owns up, either because they think it's clever or because no one honestly remembers who did it, then all the kids in the family have to cough up a quarter.

The lesson here is personal accountability. There's no tattling allowed; this is about owning up to your own oversights. If you don't, everyone pays, and frankly that's just not much fun. I've found that most kids will start owning up pretty quickly; and the number of things left on will also drastically decrease.

Naturally there's another law that takes effect here, and that's the law of hoist by your own petard. If you go out and leave a light on, or take off for the store with Willie Nelson still on the CD player, you know that kids will materialize out of nowhere, call it to your attention, and demand that you ante up. And you have to.

If a light is left on, and you might have done it, and one of the kids might have done it, and your significant other, bless his/her pointed little head, might have done it, and in all good faith no one can be really sure, then everyone has to ante up. The money from the family pool can go to family outings, family purchases, or *credit* (a family member borrowing from the pool for a special purchase). And of course this means the family meeting must formulate a *credit policy*.

Making a Credit Policy

We have a simple credit policy. A child can borrow one week's allowance ahead; he has three weeks to pay it back, with interest.

Again, we're trying to teach life skills here: responsible borrowing, responsibility for repayment of debt . . . and the value of a good credit rating.

Right, a good credit rating. We've recently added one more wrinkle to our credit policy. If your child borrows one week's allowance and repays it *with every payment absolutely on time,* it's a good mark for him in the family's credit report—that is, a section of the family journal. If he gets three good credit checks in a row, he can *increase his line of credit*—that is, he can borrow up to two weeks' allowance, with five weeks to pay it back.

Note that the payback schedule runs slightly ahead of the child's ability to make the payments out of the quick cash from his allowance. If he is going to borrow, he needs to have an extra odd job or two lined up to make up the difference.

If a child loses her credit rating by being late on a loan, she'll have to go on a probation period. Your family can determine this: two or three months is probably good for younger school-agers, six months for older children.

If she has an unblemished credit rating, reward her at the age of fourteen with a *secured credit card.* That's a first step toward establishing credit in the outside world: to get one, you deposit a sum of money, say, $500 in the bank, and you're given a $500 line of credit. It's no risk for the bank, because if you don't pay off your card on time, they can just take your deposit; but it develops a credit history for you . . . or, in this case, your child.

If your child has lost his family credit at one time but worked to get it back, he can still get the secured credit card, but he'll have to wait a little longer—perhaps till fifteen.

Here are a few forms you can use. These can be kept with the family journal, and when a loan has been negotiated and the forms filled out, they become part of the family journal.

"Amount Due" is each payment on the loan, broken out into *Principal, Interest,* and *Total.* "Date" is the date each payment is due. Put a bold line (under the third row on this table) under the final payment for

Family Bank Loan Form

I, _____(name)_____, have borrowed $_____

from _____(family name)_____ on ____(date)____ .

The interest rate is _____% p.a. (per annum.)

Payments are to be made as follows:

Principal   Interest   Date

I will pay a loan penalty of $___(amount)___ if any payment is late by more than two days.

Borrower's signature _____

Lender's signature _____(recorder for family journal)_____

Family Credit Report: Matt

Amount Due			Date	Payment		Good	Line of Credit	Lost Credit
Princ.	Interest	Total		On Time	Late			
CERTIFICATE: Matt is entitled to a secured credit card at age_____								

each loan. If the payment is on time, check the "On Time" box; if it's late, put the number of days late in the "Late" box.

Check off the "Good" box for each loan that is paid in full on time; after your child has reached the agreed-upon number of good checks, write in his new "Line of Credit" (for example, two weeks' allowance).

If your child defaults, he loses his credit for an agreed-upon period. The date until which his credit is lost goes in the "Lost Credit" box.

It's a good exercise to have your children figure out what the real interest rate would be. In the adult world this is a good thing for them to know—again, they have to remember that money costs money. The natural consequence of borrowing is that you have to pay for it.

Give your kids some problems in figuring out interest. Here's a worksheet for them:

1. You borrow $5,000 for one year at 5 percent interest rate and pay back interest and principal at the end of the year. How much do you pay back?

$$\$5,000 \times .05 \times \frac{360}{360} = \$250$$

Total payment = $5,250

2. You borrow $5,000 for six months at 6 percent interest rate and pay back interest and principal at the end of six months. How much do you pay back?

$$\$5,000 \times .06 \times \frac{180}{360} = \$150$$

Total payment = $5,150

3. You borrow $5,000 for one year at 7 percent interest rate and pay back half after six months and the other half at the end of the year. How much do you pay back?

$$\$5,000 \times .07 \times \frac{180}{360} = \$175 \text{ for first six months}$$

Payment first 6 months = $2,675

$2,500   .07 $\frac{180}{360}$ $87.50 for second six months

Payment second six months = $2,587.50

Total payment = $5,262.50

Now let's figure the same thing for a $10 loan for a year and then for thirty days, based on a 5 percent interest rate.

$$\$10 \times .05 \times \frac{360}{360} = \$50 \text{ for one year}$$

$$\$10 \times .05 \times \frac{30}{360} = \$.04 \text{ for one month}$$

That makes the interest for each week your child has borrowed $10 to be one penny, which is too small to be meaningful, certainly too small to teach anything. As we arbitrarily raised the interest rate for the savings jars, we have to raise it for family bank loans, too. The figure I recommend is in line with the savings interest from the jars chapter—slightly higher, of course, because interest on a loan is always going to be higher than interest from savings.

For loans of $1–$10: $.10 per week
For loans of $10–$20: $.20 per week

The interest goes into the family bank.

You might want to put your kids to work once they understand the principle here, figuring out how much interest they'd have to pay on a credit card or an auto loan for a used car. Give them an actual monthly statement from your own car loan and let them figure out the interest.

Incidentally, if your child comes up with a figure that doesn't jibe with the figure on the statement, don't assume she's wrong. Have her double-check the figures, and double-check them yourself. It's not that unusual for mortgages and car loans to have been calculated incorrectly. P.S. If your child can save you some money this way, you might want to split it with her as a bonus.

If there is to be a family money pool, and a family vote on how to spend it, then it follows logically that the family can also vote *not* to spend it. Then saving becomes as viable an option as spending, and that becomes a possible family decision, as do any number of *saving strategies*. Is there $50 in the budget for a family outing—say, a trip to the movies, including popcorn and soda and transportation costs? Does everyone want to spend it that way, or might there be a better idea—a video and homemade pizza, and the rest of the money goes back into the pot for basketball tickets next month, or an educational trip to Washington, D.C., next spring, or a week in Europe three years from now?

Do you want to use the money to set up a family investment club? This is another possibility. Does the family want to buy a stock or invest in a mutual fund?

This can be the big-kid version of the cereal game—a chance for one or more family members to research an investment and report back to the family (I'll discuss teaching teenagers about the stock market in a later chapter).

When you form a family investment club, you should consider that you won't be *this* family unit forever—teenagers grow up and move out, become adults, start their own families. Take this into account when you think about the liquidity of your investments.

Our family bank is a trip fund that doubles as an emergency fund. We contribute to it in all the ways I've discussed above. The family votes on where we'll take our trips and vacations, after we've done our research on what we can afford with the money we've saved. If a real emergency comes up and we have to dip into the family bank for it, then we may have to rebudget the trip and cut some things out.

We keep our trip fund in a savings account. If the amount of money in the account goes over $2,000, we invest the extra money in mutual funds.

My friend Eli, who is from Jamaica, told me about *su-su*, the Jamaican "family banking" custom that takes in a much larger extended family.

A group of Jamaicans who know each other well and trust each other—because of working together or living together in the same neighborhood—will come together to form a *partnership*. Every week everyone in the partnership will contribute a certain amount of money—$10 or $20, say—out of his paycheck, to a pool held by a banker--this role goes to an especially respected member of the community. There may be thirty or more people in the partnership.

Then, each week the entire bank goes to one member of the partnership. Everyone takes turns, so that by the end of a cycle, everyone has gotten his turn to get a large sum of money. If you were in a partnership with thirty people, and everyone put in $20, then once in every thirty weeks you would get $600. You wouldn't be making any money on the deal, of course, but you'd have $600, all at one time, that you might not have been able to save up without the encouragement and support of your partners. It's very much the equivalent of medium-term savings.

Eli says that many partnerships add another wrinkle—a *draw*. At the beginning of each cycle the banker puts numbered slips of paper in a hat—one for each member of the partnership. Everyone draws a number, and that determines the order in which that cycle's payout is made.

This is a working-class custom, and it could be argued that it leaves out one aspect of financial responsibility—getting a return on investment, learning how to use money to make money. But it emphasizes some very important community values, including trust and a spirit of community. It brings people together. It makes saving a lot easier.

The first time I heard about this, I didn't quite get it. I thought it was a lottery, and I was all set to disapprove. Actually there is an element of lottery in the draw, but it doesn't hurt anyone. It adds an element of excitement to the transaction and makes more of a game out of it—but it remains a solid communal investment plan, where everyone wins.

I've talked about saving the family money pool instead of spending it, and I always encourage saving as a life skill. As Americans we don't do nearly enough of it. But keep in mind that this is a family decision, and none of these choices are automatically better than others. Maybe your family gets a tremendous feeling of togetherness from those movie trips every other week and talking about the movie afterward over an ice cream. A family meeting gives you the opportunity to weigh the pros and cons of all these various options.

Keep in mind that you're not always going to agree unanimously as a family, and there are various ways of dealing with that. A simple "majority rules" is only one of them, and not always the fairest.

You can use the family meeting to establish more flexible rules and teach subtler civics lessons in participatory democracy and the art of compromise. You can explain to your kids that in the Congress of the United States, they have to work together and get along as best they can, and often that means modifying a bill to give partial satisfaction to the minority party. In your household you have to work together even more closely, and getting along is *really* important. So if—to use the movie example again—four of you like the idea of saving money with the video and one of you really loves going out to the mall, it doesn't mean that he has to be voted down every time. You can agree to compromise and go out to the movies once a month.

Work for Pay and Your School-ager

Your school-age child continues the work-for-pay system you've started her on as a three-year-old but takes on more responsibility.

Your toddler did her little chores but didn't really take responsibility for them. You were there to guide her through them, to say, "Come on, now, let's dust the table," then to help her find the dustcloth, to watch and point out if she'd missed a corner, and then to go with her and check off the right box on the job chart.

That's not to say that a four-year-old isn't capable of doing the job right the first time and remembering to do it without being told—children develop differently, and some of them learn faster than others. If your little one gets up every morning and does his chore before you even come down for breakfast, that's wonderful, and you can shower him with praise, but you aren't going to expect it of him or penalize him for not doing it. When your child gets to school age, he's ready to take on that new level of responsibility.

You can allow for a certain amount of leeway here. You know your own child; and, once again, children develop differently. Many kindergarteners will be able to follow this regimen; every first-grader ought to be able to. And of course, if you're starting this program for the first time with older children, that's all right, too. The younger ones may have different levels of maturity; the older ones may be set in their ways and find it harder to change; but everyone can do it.

The thing is, though, that the beginning of a school year is such a milestone in a kid's life, it really is the best time for new beginnings. So—given that if it doesn't work out right away, it's not the end of the world, and you keep trying—plan to begin these new rules with the start of kindergarten.

The new rules are these:

Jobs become harder. It's not just dusting one table anymore. Your kindergartner should be responsible for three jobs a week. These may include once-a-week and multiple-times-a-week jobs; they should certainly include both indoor and outdoor jobs (where possible) and jobs that teach a variety of life skills (not gender biased).

Three times a week is not written in stone. It should be more than one—it should be a real *list* of chores. And if your proud five-year-old says, "Hey, this is nothing—I can do more easily!" then give him more.

Here are some jobs that are appropriate for a five-year-old:

> *Dusting one room*
> *Taking out the garbage*—for a five-year-old this breaks down into any *one* of a number of smaller chores:
>> collecting trash from the wastebaskets
>> separating recyclables
>> stacking newspapers and magazines
>> taking garbage out to the curb if you live in a suburb or the hall if you live in an apartment
>
> *Weeding one flower bed*
> *Watering the plants* (outdoors or indoors)
> *Brushing the snow off the family car*
> Washing the TV set (that's what we call it—it means dusting the TV screen with a damp cloth; you don't actually have to throw the TV set in the washer, which is just as well, because then you'd have to separate out the color from the black-and-white TVs)

School kids become responsible for their own jobs. You don't stay with your child and talk her through the job anymore: she'll do it on her own. And you don't remind her to do it every day, either; she's responsible for remembering, for finding the time, and for doing the job properly.

School kids become responsible for their own job charts. Here's the way a sample job chart looks for a school-ager.

Kyle's Job Chart
June

Clean kitty litter (3x a week)*	K M/D				
Brush cats (every other day)	K M/D				
Water plants (every other day)	K M/D				
Clean up around trampoline (every other day)	K M/D				
Dust living room, dining room, family room (2x a week)	K M/D				
Do laundry (2x a week)	K M/D				

Remember, your child is no longer a toddler who has to be told what to do and how to do it every time. Now she's taking responsibility for her own work.

You're the boss, and that carries certain responsibilities, too: the responsibility to state the job clearly, the responsibility to assess the efficiency of your employees, and the responsibility to maintain good employer/employee communication.

You'll explain, when you introduce a new chore, exactly what it is, how to do it, and how often it has to be done. If the child doesn't get it right away, or forgets a detail, she can always ask later, and you'll be available (and supportive, naturally—this is still a parent-child relationship, as well as management-labor).

You'll give a time estimate. This is helpful to the child in planning her week, and it also is something of a guard against dawdling.

You'll have the child repeat the task to you—the scope of the job, the instructions for doing it, the estimated time—so you can be sure you both understand what's required.

On Kyle's job chart above, here's what I expect:

Clean kitty litter: We have four cats, so this *has* to be done three times a week. The job description includes emptying out the old litter into a garbage bag, sweeping up around the box, taking the bag out to the garbage, putting new litter in the box, putting away the kitty litter bag.

The asterisk next to "Clean kitty litter" on the chart indicates that this is a *shared chore*—Kyle and Rhett do it together.

This started out as their idea—they came to me and asked if they could share the chore, because it was hard for either of them to lift the fifty-pound kitty litter bag alone.

I agreed to let them try it, and I came to think of it as a good idea, if you have more than one child, to assign some shared chores along with the individual jobs. This teaches cooperation, sharing of responsibility, and a different way of looking at the time value of money: bartering time. It's up to the kids themselves to work out with each other what it's worth if one covers for the other (agreed upon in advance) in a shared job.

If two kids of very different ages are sharing a job, it's probably a good idea to give the older one the responsibility of making sure the younger one pulls his weight but isn't stuck with too much responsibility.

Brush cats: This is to some extent a judgment call—brush the cats until you've got all the excess hair off them, so they don't shed. It's hard for an eleven-year-old to ascertain exactly what that means, so the job description is "Brush each cat for five minutes."

This is a job that involved some training at first, so before I left Kyle alone with it, I worked with her for a few weeks. I had to teach her the basic brush stroke for getting the hair off a cat without getting the cat mad, and I had to teach her specific techniques for dealing with individual cats. Stanley, for example, doesn't like to be brushed one little bit, and approaching her requires some special diplomacy.

Now, of course, Kyle knows more about brushing the cats than I do.

Water plants: This one is fairly simple. Take a watering can and walk around the plant in a circular pattern, emptying the contents of the can at a measured rate, the object being the saturation of the ground around the plant.

Clean up around trampoline: One of our recent family fund expenses was a large trampoline. It's good for adults with bad backs . . . and, of course, kids don't need that excuse.

A large trampoline has to be kept outside, and the outdoors is full of things like trees and birds that tend to drop objects on big, flat, inviting surfaces like trampolines. So for both aesthetics and maintenance (oak leaves and guano are both kind of acidic and could eat away at the surface of the trampoline), someone has to sweep it every day and work on a few spots with a scrub brush.

Dust living room, dining room, family room: This seems simple, but there have to be ground rules to make it fair for Kyle. Right now my work space is still spread out over a couple of tables in the living room and family room. This makes dusting those tables a real impossibility. She dusts the areas that fall within the broad category of "neat to start with," meaning if someone left a priceless Super Bowl football autographed by Joe Montana on the table, you'd be able to find it.

Do laundry: Kyle is eleven, so this job is more demanding than if she was four, less demanding than if she was fourteen. For a toddler, doing the laundry might mean measuring out the detergent and putting it in the machine. For a teenager, it could include getting the laundry out of all the hampers and schlepping it downstairs. For now, it means separate whites from colors, load the washer, add the detergent, run the washer, transfer the clothes from the washer to the dryer, run the dryer.

I make folding the laundry a separate chore.

No work, no pay. At the end of the week your child checks off every job she's completed, in the box next to her initial.

But that, of course, is only half the story. It's not enough for her to be satisfied that she's done the job; you have to be satisfied, too. That's why there's a second box, for Mom or Dad to check off.

If all the chores are not completed and checked off, there's no allowance for that week.

We'll stop for a second on this one, because this is the rule that strikes many people—adults as well as kids—as unfair. But think about it for a minute. If you were on a job in the real world, and you walked off in the middle of the week and left the job half finished, would you expect to be able to go back at the end of the week and get paid for half the job?

You shouldn't.

And kids won't, either.

Well, they won't if they're used to it. When I talked about this rule on

The Oprah Winfrey Show, Rhett was with me. When Oprah turned to Rhett, registering the audience's disbelief, and asked him: "I don't get this—you mean if you don't do every single job, you don't get paid anything at all?" Rhett looked up at her, put his hands on his hips, and said proudly: "No work, no pay. That's the way it works."

Oprah spontaneously hugged him for it. My little boy won the hearts of ten million people at that moment and his mother's most of all.

If your kids are older, and you're just starting this regimen with them—well then, frankly, they probably will complain about this rule. At first. The answer to that is, "A rule is a rule." This is a good rule, and it works, and most important, it reinforces important values. You don't want your kids to get into the habit of thinking in terms of cutting corners on work or making little bargains in their minds along the lines of "Well, I can get away with fulfilling only part of my obligations."

No work, no pay is at the very heart of the whole philosophy of using financial responsibility to teach value responsibility.

I've mentioned that you should no longer have to keep after your school-agers constantly with reminders to do their chores. How often should you keep after them?

The "three strikes and you're out" rule is a good one here. Three warnings a week is plenty. More than that and it becomes nagging, which is wearing on you and counterproductive. That's three warnings a week total, not for each chore.

If you don't stay on top of them every day, how will you know if they've done their chores?

You'll know. For one thing, kids mostly tend to make a production of it when they do things. For another, you're the parent, and you live there, too. If the cats don't get brushed, I always know it because there's cat hair all over the house. If the furniture isn't dusted, I know because by the end of the week I can write a note to Kyle on the end table saying something endearing like "No Work, No Pay." I know if the kids are watering the plants because in our case the plants are a couple of young saplings down at the end of the driveway, and the job involves filling a watering can and lugging it down, which is a very noticeable sort of endeavor. And if the litter box doesn't get emptied, my nose tells me.

In fact, as I write this, my nose just gave me a message that said "No allowance for Kyle and Rhett this week."

This is, I hasten to point out, a very rare happenstance for my kids. But it does happen. They goofed off. They knew it. And they had to live with the consequences.

They also, by the way, had to change the litter box. There was a behavioral punishment as well as a monetary one.

Because the litter box was a shared job, it was a shared responsibility, and that meant they both suffered the penalty. I didn't ask whose fault it was that the litter hadn't been changed; that really wasn't my business. It was between them.

However, if you set up shared chores, and one of the partners in the job is consistently letting the other one down, the one who's getting stuck has a right to complain.

A family meeting is a good place to air the complaint, and a situation like this would justify calling a special family meeting where the problem can be talked out and a solution arrived at—perhaps simply no more shared chores for a while.

While we're on the subject of charts, there's one more that I recommend putting up on your refrigerator, a chart that everyone needs and probably none of us get enough of—a chart for pure positive reinforcement. I call this one the "proud chart," and it deserves a place on your refrigerator right there next to the job charts.

The principle behind the proud chart is simple. Each child has one. Each week she writes on it one thing about herself she's proud of. It can be anything—tried extra hard in soccer practice, assembled a swing set for baby brother, passed a chemistry test. Everyone has something to be proud of, and it's important to let your children know they have a right to be proud of themselves.

Citizen of the Household
Chores and Odd Jobs

By the time your child reaches school age, gold star charts for Citizen of the Household chores start to seem a little babyish, and in fact they are a little babyish. It's probably time to get rid of them—if not with your kindergartener, at least with your first-grader. This is a little like toilet training or weaning to a cup—some children will need it longer than others.

But the point is, you're moving to a new framework in which the performing of Citizen of the Household chores is expected. They're part of *being* a Citizen of the Household.

You do want to remember that any time you're instituting a "rite of passage" like this, where the kids are outgrowing something they've grown to feel good about, make sure you don't surprise them with it. Make sure there's plenty of preparation. "When you start kindergarten [or first grade, or whatever], and you're a big boy, there'll be all sorts of changes. You'll be able to stay up fifteen minutes later at night. And you'll be too old for the gold star chart, so we'll stop using it. Instead, you'll have new jobs you can do to make extra money."

As your kids get older, their responsibility for chores (work for pay) increases. Their pay increases, of course: pay for age means a dollar-a-week pay increase each birthday. And you'll also start giving them the opportunity to earn extra money by doing odd jobs.

Okay, so now we have three different categories of jobs: work-for-pay chores, Citizen of the Household chores, and odd jobs. Is this going to get confusing? And is it really necessary?

I believe it shouldn't be *too* confusing—and in some very important ways it can eliminate confusion. And it is necessary.

That's because, as we all know, kids test limits and possibilities every chance they get. After they've assimilated the concept of work for pay, it doesn't take long before they start wondering what else they can get paid for, and that's when you hear that familiar parental plaint, "All of a sudden he wants to be paid for everything he does."

If you have your work-for-pay chore chart and your odd job list, then you have an absolutely clear set of rules to cover that issue. You get paid for the jobs on those two lists; you don't get paid for anything else.

How do you divide up the chores among these three lists?

It's an inexact science.

You can pretty much do it any way you want to, within certain general guidelines.

All *personal* jobs (like cleaning your room) are Citizen of the Household chores. You should *never* pay a child for cleaning his room, or brushing his teeth, or cleaning up the sink after he finishes using it, or folding and putting away his own clean laundry. And the personal jobs don't get rotated—everyone is always responsible for his own personal stuff.

Beyond that, there's no real difference between work-for-pay chores and Citizen of the Household chores. Both come from the generally defined list of chores that absolutely need to be done to keep the household running smoothly. You separate out a few of them to create the work-for-pay structure, which is important, but there's no special reason why changing the kitty litter should be work for pay and loading and emptying the dishwasher should be Citizen of the Household, instead of vice versa.

For both categories you should rotate chores among your kids, so that you remain an equal opportunity life skill instructor.

If chores are essential to the running of the household, odd jobs are household enhancing. They fall into two categories.

The first includes things you need to do, or pay someone else to do, but things aren't going to fall apart if they don't get done this week or even next week. "Washing the dog" would be an example.

The second are large jobs that, when they need to be done, actually do need to be done right away, but they're seasonal jobs, nothing you could put on a regular job chart—and they tend to be so big that you'd feel it was a little bit of an imposition just to dump them on a kid without paying him something. "Shoveling snow off the driveway" is an example of this sort of job.

Here's a list of chores I post as Citizen of the Household chores:

Personal

Put clothes in hamper
Divide whites and colors for laundry
Keep room reasonably neat (you define this; for me, the bottom
    line is if it's free of breeding diseases)
Sort, fold, and put away clothes

Household

Set table
Clear table
Fill dishwasher
Empty dishwasher and put away dishes
Sort garbage (organic for compost, recyclable, and so on)
In charge of "mending bin"—sew buttons, mend small tears in
    clothes*
Purge refrigerator of any food wearing an angora sweater
Empty refrigerator, clean out and wash shelves

And here's a list of what I consider odd jobs:

Mow lawn
Wash cars
Wax cars
Pick up and return videos
Label and stack videos
"Librarian"—organize books by category and author
Put family pictures in album
Wash dog
Weed garden
Shovel snow off driveway
Clean snow off cars

*You can make this a personal chore, but I feel that leaves the decision on when some-
thing needs to be mended far too much in the hands of someone who feels a complete set
of buttons are considerably less important than I do. This way, mending becomes another life skill that everyone learns.

Clean garbage cans
Paint porch furniture
Regrout tiles
Clean inside of car
Rake leaves
Sweep walk/driveway
Scrub tiles/bathroom

The odd job chart goes up on the refrigerator next to chore charts, and it includes the job; the fee for the job (based on a reasonable hourly rate) and the estimated hours needed for completion; a space for your kid to sign up and indicate when he expects to do the job; a space for the kid to check off that the job has been completed; a space for you to check off that it's been completed to your satisfaction.

This constitutes a work contract of sorts. You've identified the job and the compensation for it; your child has committed to undertake it; you've stipulated, and he has agreed, that the job must be completed to your satisfaction.

That chart would look like this:

JOB	FEE	RATE	SCHEDULED	WORKER	DONE	OK
Mow lawn	$5	1.25 hrs. @ $4 hr.	Sat eve.	Matt	X	X
Wash cars	$4	1hr. @ $4 hr.	Sun. aft.	Rachel	X	X
Pick up and return videos	$1	(spare time job)	Wed aft. Thurs aft.	Rachel	X	X
Clean basement	$30	6 hrs. @ $5 hr.	Sun	Matt/ Rachel		

A few more notes on odd jobs. They mean more money in your child's pocket, so don't be surprised if she has a tendency, all things being equal, to gravitate toward the odd job list first.

But all things can't be equal. Odd jobs are a kind of privilege, and they *have* to be scheduled into a hierarchy of time budgeting. Before your child can take on an odd job, she must have completed the following:

Personal obligations: This means personal grooming and room maintenance, but it also—very important, nonnegotiable—means homework. Homework comes before any other task.

Citizen obligations: In addition to Citizen of the Household chores, this category includes any commitment your child has undertaken—either a commitment that's being paid for, like guitar or karate lessons, or any commitment she's made to others—and these can be as diverse as basketball practice or delivering meals to AIDS patients.

Allowance obligations: These are the work-for-pay chores.

If your kid is planning a seriously odd job–oriented summer, when there is no homework, you'll still want to work with her in arranging a schedule.

In addition to the odd job chart, it's good to have a stack of odd job contracts made up and ready. You can put them in a box, or in/out boxes, near where you have the chart. The contracts can be simple. I use one like this:

Odd Job Contract

_____ will complete _____
(name)   (job)

by _____ and get paid _____ .
        (date)   (amount)

_____
(worker signature)

_____
(employer signature)

_____
(date)

After you've finished figuring out an acceptable hourly rate for a task, it's your responsibility to price out the job. Estimate the number of hours you think it would take an average unskilled worker to complete the work. Multiply by the hourly rate.

Post the task, and the per-task payment, on your odd job chart. Always pay by the task, not by the hour. If your child finishes the job in a much shorter time than it would have taken that theoretical average unskilled worker—and the job is done to your satisfaction—that's his bonus.

Once your child has proved his reliability doing odd jobs at home, he can branch out into the neighborhood and start soliciting jobs from others, by asking friends of the family, by knocking on doors (if it's that kind of neighborhood), by leaving fliers in mailboxes or tucked under the windshield wipers of cars, by posting an ad for his services in the local supermarket or wherever there's a bulletin board. You and he can discuss the relative effectiveness of these techniques. In general, the direct, person-to-person approach is likely to be the most effective. If he's going to use an ad, make it an eye-catching one.

Make sure your child is legally qualified to do the kind of work she's looking for. Most odd jobs for neighbors—yardwork, washing windows, and the like—are not covered by child labor laws, but be sure to check state and local laws to find out if working papers are needed.

Odd jobs don't have to be limited to cutting the neighbor's grass. My friends and I have hired enterprising kids, at one time or another, to tutor our own children in chess, lacrosse, art—even to teach the alphabet to little ones or to read to them in a neighborhood story hour.

Kids can start their own businesses. I had a neat one when I was ten. I lived in West Caldwell, New Jersey, a town with a storm sewer system that I explored like a spelunker in Carlsbad Caverns. When I knew my way through it thoroughly, I went into business giving sewer tours to the younger children in the neighborhood, for a quarter a tour.

I admit, though, that I had a devilish turn of mind as a ten-year-old. I would take the little kids into the sewers, tell them ghost stories and frighten them silly, then charge them another dime apiece to lead them back out.

I also did rock painting. I invented this business myself, after I had asked my mother what those colored balls were on the shelf of her friend's living room.

"They're paperweights, dear," my mother explained. "People put them on piles of paper to hold them down."

"They pay money for heavy blobs you put on top of a pile of paper? How much?"

She explained that people might pay up to $500 for some of these, because they were "collectibles," and my mind started whirring. I knew that I wasn't going to get $500 a heavy blob out of this, but I suspected I could probably get something.

I was looking for a business with very little overhead, because I didn't have very much money, and what I did have I didn't want to spend. This seemed like the perfect thing for me.

I invested in some paint and some brushes and set about finding rocks that were smooth and pretty and about the size of paperweights. Beach rocks were the best. I made up my first bunch and took them down to a local boutique, where they agreed to take them on consignment. Amazingly enough, there turned out to be a real market for paperweights created by an eleven-year-old, and I had a successful summer. I sold about fifty rocks, made $200, and put every penny of it (I was a saver) into my college fund.

Labor and Management

Labor-management relationships are always ticklish, whether they involve families, or hospital workers, or major league baseball players. One does the best one can to make them fair and harmonious. As a general rule, I don't recommend negotiating a price for odd jobs, especially with school-agers. They do quite enough negotiating as it is; and you are, after all, still the parent.

If you do your homework and set fair pay schedules for odd jobs, there shouldn't be a problem here. If there is, you can count on the law of the marketplace to reveal it to you. If there are some jobs your kids never sign up for, there's a good chance you haven't made the offer attractive enough.

However, with the best will in the world, you can still goof up. Sometimes you can severely miscalculate the difficulty of the job.

Here again, use your best judgment, and remember that the best boss is the fairest boss. Suppose your kids come to you and say, "Hey, you calculated four hours for that basement job, and we worked our . . . well, we worked our elbows off [you are still their parents, after all], and it still took us ten hours—and we did a great job."

You know your kids. If they have a track record of honesty and good work, renegotiate the job.

Your children can also develop their own skills and bid for household contracts, anything from plumbing, to cooking gourmet appetizers for your business entertaining, to electronic repairs.

As we move into the computer age, many of us are finding that we have children who are a lot more computer literate than we are. One of your kids might want to bid for the job of transferring all your household bookkeeping to Quicken (or some other bookkeeping/accounting program) and keeping it up on a monthly basis.

I have a friend who directs a small nonprofit organization. Her teenage son designed a modification to her mail-merge program that saves her several hours a month on the organization's monthly mailings. This created a new family work situation . . . and new lessons in how money is transacted, in the time value of money and time, and in fair exchange of value. My friend decided to pay her son a *royalty*—a stipend every month that reflected the time and money she was continuing to save because of this onetime but ingenious idea of his.

The First Children's Bank, which I started at FAO Schwarz in New York, was Kyle's brainchild, and I gave her full credit for it. She was five years old at the time. I made her a consultant and gave her business cards with her name on them, and I gave her a dollar each time she helped me with the project.

She went with me to a convention of bankers in Miami and even gave a speech, explaining how she had come up with the idea for The First Children's Bank. She had to stand on a chair to reach the microphone.

Later I saw her surrounded by a group of bankers, proudly exchanging business cards with them and telling them about her one-dollar salary. And not long after that, she and a group of very distinguished gentlemen approached me, and she informed me that they had offered her fifty dollars, and she was going to work for them.

After a bit of negotiation—and she had a very powerful negotiation team on her side—we reached a compromise. We agreed that if she moved to Atlanta to take this other position, she'd miss too much school (and I'd miss her too much). We settled on a raise to ten dollars.

If your kids are labor and you're management, do they have the right to strike?

No.

I like the labor-management analogy in talking about structuring your household's chores and responsibilities because it spotlights a lot of kids' rights, but this is one you can't give them.

For one thing, the household can't be shut down by a strike. Dishes have to be washed, laundry done, meals prepared, pets fed, and goodness knows litter boxes have to be emptied.

For another, things should never have to get so far out of hand that a strike would be justified. This isn't a widget factory, it's your home, and it's populated by people who love each other and who, underneath it all, want to live together in harmony.

Arbitration, on the other hand, is an acceptable family labor-management tool.

Use your family meeting to set up a format for arbitration and negotiation. If a grandparent or an aunt or uncle is available as an arbitrator, that can work. Just remember two things: first, a little humor, a little tolerance, and a lot of love and understanding can resolve most family disputes; and second, the humor shouldn't all be directed at the kids. If they want to arbitrate a labor dispute, this is another valuable lesson in life skills, and you don't want to patronize them. Kids take themselves seriously, and they have a right to. If you enter into arbitration with your nine-year-old, it's not "cute," it's real. Make sure to set it up so the arbitration becomes a win-win situation; you give a little, they give a little, and a good lesson is learned about the value of arbitration as a life skill.

Labor arbitration may involve shorter hours (in family terms this generally relates to finding a balance between what they want to do and what you think they need to do) or better working conditions (perhaps they feel that you're not providing them sufficiently up-to-date equipment for doing their chores). In a family situation they're not likely to involve benefits—those are all built in to being part of the family.

Then, of course, there's the big labor-management issue: more pay.

How much should you pay for odd jobs? This is a question to be taken seriously and decided on a job-by-job basis.

One basic rule of thumb is "Don't pay too much, and don't pay too little." That seems obvious, but it bears some thinking about, and there are reasons for avoiding both extremes.

Paying too little for odd jobs creates the same problem as paying too little for allowance: it teaches the lesson that working isn't worth the time expended on it.

Paying too much sends an equally unrealistic message. You're not compensating your kids for what they've done. Instead you're doing something else: you're paying to show them how much you love them or to assuage your guilt at not spending enough time with them or something like that.

This is wrong. As simple as that. Wrong. Give your kids love to show them how much you love them. That's ample, and it's also the only thing that will do the job. If you feel guilty about not spending enough time with them, rearrange your schedule to spend more time with them. That may not be possible over the short run, but over the long run there's always a way.

In addition, make sure that whenever you use money, it's always in the service of teaching a lesson in the fair exchange of values.

Do a little research. A professional lawn service, for example, will get about $25 per man hour. So if you try to hire your twelve-year-old to do the same job for a dollar an hour, you could be asking for trouble. For one thing, she has access to the same research sources that you do. She can call up a lawn service and ask them what they get.

Here's a sounder approach—fairer for everyone, in the long run, and a good learning experience in the value of money. Include your child in the process of research to determine a fair price.

Mowing lawns is a common job that kids hire out to do. So we asked a professional—John Podmayerski of Lawns and Homes in Saugerties, New York, how much he charges. John, who services private homes and businesses, charges an average of $25 an hour for his services, although he usually charges per job, not per hour.

So your twelve-year-old has called Lawns and Homes and discovered they get $25 an hour for their services, and she's checked the odd job chart and noticed that you're offering four bucks. Strike time?

Not quite yet. Let's look at what happens to that $25 once it leaves your hand and goes into the bank account of the lawn service. John broke it down for us:

Lawn Service Expenses Based on $25 Per Man Hour

Expense	% of total	$ amount
Equipment	24.8	6.20
Office/business	8.6	2.15
Employees (wages, employer's portion of FICA, workmen's comp)	33.7	8.43
Totals	67.1	16.78
Balance	32.9	8.22

So that $8.22 per hour is the lawn service person's net—not including, John points out, bookkeeping time (as a small-business owner, he does his own books—a larger operation would have to hire a bookkeeper and make that part of the overhead), time spent estimating and bidding on jobs, miscellaneous time with customers, and equipment maintenance and repair time.

There's also the matter of acquired expertise. For lawn repair, for example, John has to know not only the area that needs to be covered with topsoil and grass seed, but how thick the topsoil has to be spread and the quality and consistency of both soil and seed that will work in a certain area.

Then you have to consider that your calculation of $4 an hour is based on an average unskilled laborer's ability, not experienced professional skills. If your twelve-year-old is twice as efficient as average, she's working at the level of an experienced professional, and her wages are going to be right up there. Don't forget you're paying by the task, not by the hour. If your twelve-year-old is twice as efficient as the average, she'll finish the job in half the time—and then she's making $8 an hour.

Labor and management sound like rough concepts to introduce into the domestic harmony of a loving family. They conjure up some unnerving associations—is your twelve-year-old daughter going to turn into John L. Lewis?

But we know that the most loving of families can sometimes become a battlefield. Tensions, misunderstandings, and divergent goals are part of any household, and any negotiating tool that can help to bridge those misunderstandings is a good one.

After all, once you set up a system whereby you put your kids to work for pay, you *are* management and they *are* labor. And the more negotiating procedures you have in place, in this or any other realm of potential conflict, the better your chance for conflict resolution.

Need Vs. Want

Spending is the first financial concept your kids are going to understand—it comes naturally, as soon as kids learn what money is. Saving, investing, and charity have to be taught.

Differentiating between different kinds of spending has to be taught as well. Babies don't understand the difference between need vs. want—if they want it, they need it. This distinction has to be taught as well, and the lesson has to be repeated and reinforced over and over.

Frankly, it's never an easy one. We all contain within us that child who screams, "I want! I want!" He never disappears completely—in fact, I call this the "I want! I want!" syndrome. And no matter how old we get, those "I want!" cries can be very strong at times, strong enough that we experience them as overpowering: "If I don't get that new car, I'll just die!" And of course, if you were literally going to die from not getting the car, you'd certainly need it.

We have to train that critical facility that allows us to distinguish between need and want. The more we do, the more alert we're going to be to the distinction. The "need vs. want game" can be played in the car, in a family meeting, in the mall, even at the dinner table. It's a good way to develop that critical facility and to keep it in shape.

Start with broad categories, for example:

Needs	Wants
Food	CD player
Clothes	Rollerblades
Medicine	Ice cream
Education	Some clothes (designer jeans, for example)

Then move on to harder choices.

The need vs. want game is a way of explaining the concept of fixed and variable expenses: the things you absolutely have to include in your budget, because there is no way of doing without them, and the things that you can prioritize according to how much money you have left in your budget after the fixed needs are met.

This is a lesson of reality, not morality, so don't teach it too harshly. It's not wrong to want things; in fact, it's great to want things. Enrichment is an important part of life. But it's important that your child know there are costs to everything, and everyone has to know how to build a budget around the cornerstone of fixed expenses.

Anyway, back to the more challenging variations of the need vs. want game: how about playing it as a car game, using billboards? It can lead to some surprising results and some lively debates.

I recently played the billboard game with my family over a ten-mile stretch of road in upstate New York. The players were Michele, a graduate student who helps me with my kids; Kyle and Rhett; and me. This is how it came out:

Miller Beer—unanimous for want.

Saab Autos—Neale, Rhett, Michele: want.
  Kyle: "It depends. You need a car—you'd have to look into it to see if you really need a Saab or not."

Shop 'n' Save Supermarkets—Michele, Rhett, Kyle: need.
  Neale: "There'd be stuff in it you'd need, and stuff in it you'd want."

Eagle Snacks (potato chips)—Rhett, Kyle, Neale: want.
  Michele: "Well, you need *some* snacks."

Middletown Times-Herald-Record (local newspaper)—Kyle:
  "You need it because you need to know what's going on."
  Rhett: "It's a want. You'd want it for stuff like movie listings or places to go, but you don't need those things."
  Michele: "It's a need. You need to know what's happening in your immediate surroundings."
  Neale: "You want it for the information it gives you. You need it to line the kitty litter box or to start a fire."

Winston cigarettes—unanimous for want.

WPDH Radio (rock station)—Kyle: "You'd want it for music, you'd need it for weather."

Rhett: "Want. It's entertainment."
Michele: "It's a want—but news and weather are important."

Anaconda Sporting Goods—Rhett: "It could be a need. If you were going to basketball camp you'd need a ball. If you were going fishing, you'd need a fishing pole."
Neale: "If you needed to fish to eat, you'd need a pole, but you wouldn't need an expensive pole. If you were a professional baseball player, you'd need a really good glove, but you probably wouldn't get it from a local sporting goods store. You'd get it from the NBA." (Chorus: "The *NBA?* For a *baseball glove?*")
Michele: "A want, for my recreational interests."
Kyle: "If you were the coach of a local team, you wouldn't be going to the NBA [snicker, snicker] for your equipment, and you'd need balls and uniforms and stuff."

Miron Lumber and Hardware—Rhett: "It's a need. You can't build with air—you need wood and tiles."
Kyle: "It's a need. If your door or window breaks, you need a new one."
Michele: "Want if it's for personal improvements around your home, need if you're a contractor."

Genesee Ice Beer—unanimous for want.

Hart Water Conditioning Systems—Kyle: "Sixty to forty percent for need. You'd need it if it was for your health; if it was just to make your water taste better, it would be a want."
Neale: "It's a want. A water conditioning system is mostly to make your clothes feel softer after you wash them."

Prestige Toyota—"You'll come for price, you'll stay for ser-vice"—Kyle: "You need good service and not to be cheated, especially if you're an older person, so if they're telling the truth, a good price and good service would be a need."

Michele: "If I had a Toyota, I'd need it for parts."

Rhett: "I'm too young. I don't need a car."

Neale: "I won't buy a foreign car, so I don't need it and I don't want it."

Callahan Stone and Asphalt Products—Neale: "No one would go into a stone and asphalt store unless they needed it."

Kyle: "You'd need it if you were a contractor. But there's something none of you are thinking of. You might not need it around here, but if you lived in Phoenix, Arizona, there are a lot of scorpions and snakes around on the ground, and you might need really good stone and asphalt paving to keep them away."

MVP Health Plan—Kyle: "It's an absolute definite need, especially if you're old and you're going to die. You need a health plan to take care of your health needs and take care of your spouse after you're gone."

Neale: "You need insurance—MVP would be an alternate choice."

Michele: "You need it—you never know what will happen."

Rhett: "If you don't have it, you need it. If you have it, you may want to change companies to get a better deal."

Neale: "I agree with Rhett."

River Aviation Flying School—Kyle: "It would probably be a want, but you might need it if you came from a long line of fliers, and it was expected of you for family reasons—or if you planned to make a career of flying."

Neale: "If it was for your livelihood, one hundred percent need. If it's for a hobby, one hundred percent want."

Mid-Hudson Auto Upholstery and Boat Tops—Michele: "Definitely a want.

Rhett: "A boat is a want, but if you have one, and you're going down the Amazon into the rain forests, you'd need a top for it."

Neale: "Need if it's your livelihood; otherwise a want."

I was surprised not only that the kids had an answer for everything, but that all their answers were thoughtful and to the point. Sue Walker, my child care adviser, pointed out that some of their answers—like the boat tops on the Amazon—show that they are aware of differences between people. Just because they don't need a boat top doesn't mean that they can't put themselves in the situation of someone who does.

Playing this game on the road is bound to be more interesting than trying to spot cows or out-of-state license plates, and its a lot more educational. It teaches the values of intellectual discussion of issues where there's no right or wrong, and this is very good for kids' self-esteem.

Kids Spending on Themselves

The basic rule on your kids' quick cash and medium-term savings is that the money is theirs, and they can spend it any way they want to.

This is the *guilt-free budget:* If your child chooses to buy something with his discretionary income (obviously this should not include alcohol or drugs or anything else that house rules don't allow), he has a right to buy it. Ultimately the only consideration is whether or not he can afford it.

You can institute some guidelines surrounding this basic rule. Ultimately the spending decision is your child's. But you can institute a cooling-off period, which will also function as a discussion period.

The cooling-off period should be a factor of the expense of object and the age of child. Of course to some extent, the time part of it alone is taken care of by the medium-term savings jar, but sometimes with gifts and odd jobs, a child's ready cash can add up. Here's a chart that can work:

Age	Price of Item	Cooling-off Period
5–8 years	$5–$10	1 week
	$10–$20	2 weeks
	$20+	3 weeks
9–12 years	$10–$20	1 week
	$20–$30	2 weeks
	$30+	3 weeks
13+ years	$20–$30	1 week
	$30–$40	2 weeks
	$40–$50	3 weeks

Along with the emotional cooling-down aspect—will that Lion King lunch box still exert the same magic appeal two weeks later, or will something new have caught your child's interest?—this waiting period can be a time for reason and discussion.

Put the contemplated purchase into a need vs. want framework—do you want it or need it? This doesn't mean beat up on the kid, make him feel bad about himself for wanting when he should be needing—there are all sorts of legitimate reasons for wanting something, but it is useful to put them in perspective.

Then have him consider the relative value of possible purchases—is the brand-name baseball glove really that much better than an off brand? Are you paying for better quality (in other words, will it be more flexible and last longer?) or just someone's advertising budget?

How long did it take to work for the item? Your kids should start to be aware of the value of their work in relation to its purchasing power. That charm bracelet costs $12? How long am I going to have to work to earn the money to buy it? If kids start thinking of the value of objects in terms of their own time and their own work, they'll start to scrutinize a lot more carefully what things cost. They'll be asking themselves not just, "Am I getting good value for my dollar?" but also, "Am I getting good value for my time?" They'll learn an important lesson in appreciating the value of what they're buying. They may even start to reconsider whether an item is really worth the price.

How long will it last? If you're going to be playing baseball from junior high through college, and the stitching on that off-brand glove is going to start unraveling after a season or two, then it may not be the best buy.

Is there upkeep or maintenance on the item? That has to be considered as part of the cost. Those portable boom boxes eat up an incredible number of batteries, and a Barbie may not be satisfying for long without Barbie's tennis outfit and Barbie's fully outfitted RV.

You're not exactly asking your child to justify or defend her guilt-free purchase; you are asking her talk over the pros and cons with you. Still, ultimately, the purchase is her decision, and once the decision is made, you must respect it. In fact, reinforce the child's right: "I'm proud of you for thinking it through and making an informed choice." If the child asks, "Would you have made the same choice?" it's all right to say, "No, I wouldn't. But you don't have to make the same choice I would."

It's your responsibility as parents to provide for your child's needs; it's his own responsibility to provide for his wants. When needs and wants are combined in one item, you can separate out the cost. If it's back-to-school time, and your kid needs a good new pair of sneakers, but he wants a pair of Reebok high-tops that pump up and glow in the dark, you can share the expense. You kick in the cost of a good (not bottom-of-the-line, but a good, well-made, long-lasting), no-frills pair of sneakers. He can take that money, add the amount of the difference, and buy the sneakers he wants.

Contracts: Borrowing, Lending, and Trading

Borrowing and Lending

Kids have their own social structure, which is characterized primarily by not having anything to do with the adult world; one of its secondary characteristics is that kids will borrow money from each other and lend money to each other.

You're not going to change this any more than you're going to convince them that the giant baggy T-shirts everyone's wearing today are nowhere near as cool as the bell-bottoms you wore when you were in high school; but when you find out that they've started in on this borrowing/lending pattern, you can use it as an opportunity for more life skill lessons.

If your child is mostly a lender, you can remind him that Shakespeare wrote, "Neither a borrower nor a lender be" (and hope that he doesn't find out that Shakespeare put those words into the mouth of an old fuddy-duddy to whom no one ever listened).

A more useful tack would be to talk to him about why he lends his money. Here are a few questions worth asking:

"How do loans to friends make you feel?"

"Why are you doing it? Do you feel you need it to make or keep friends?"

"Do you expect to get paid back? Is this a gift or a loan?"

If your child is engaging in the world of school financial transactions, this can be a good time to start giving her lessons in the meaning of verbal contracts and the art of negotiation.

This is more than just a junior business school lesson; it's a full-fledged life skills lesson. We live in an informal age, and in many ways that's a good thing. But it's important for our children to learn structure, to learn—yes, a little formality in their dealings with others.

Structure in a transaction promotes clarity. It promotes a general understanding on both sides of what has just taken place. It can forestall arguments and bad feeling later on, and it promotes a sense of self-confidence and empowerment.

Borrowing and lending is often an embarrassing situation. The person who's borrowing is embarrassed to ask for it; the person who's lending is embarrassed to ask what the borrower expects the terms of the loan to be.

If another child asks your child to borrow money, he doesn't have to say yes. It's an important part of his self-empowerment to be able to say no to a friend—either because he doesn't have the money, he can't afford to have it tied up for as long as the friend will need it, or he doesn't approve of what the friend will use it for (to buy drugs, for example). It is perfectly legitimate for him to ask the following questions:

1. How much do you want to borrow?
2. Why do you need the money?
3. When will you pay it back?

Talk to your child about these situations. Talk her through some hypothetical situations: What would you do if . . . ? Do some role-playing.

In fact, because this is one of the most difficult social situations your child will face, role-playing can help tremendously to rehearse her for facing these situations when and if they happen.

Tad and I did it with Kyle recently, and we discovered just what a stressful situation this really is. Kyle is bright, outgoing, and irrepressible and always eager to participate in any of the games and workshops I set up; but this one was different. Tad and I played the roles of different friends asking to borrow money from her, and even though it was just a game, the stress showed on her immediately. She shrank on her chair, her voice shrank to a whisper. But she handled both situations in an incredibly responsible way.

In the first one, I played a selfish, manipulative friend named Jane, who doesn't need the money.

"Hey, Kyle, can I borrow fifty dollars? I really need it."

"What's it for, Janie?"

"There's this really cool denim jacket. . . ."

"Why not use your own money?"

"Oh, I don't want to. I need all my money. I'm saving up for a computer. But this jacket is so neat. . . ."

"Why not ask your parents?"

"I don't want them to know. It's none of their business."

The next question on *my* list is "When will you pay it back?" We hadn't coached Kyle at all on this. We hadn't told her she was supposed to ask any of the three questions mentioned earlier.

She never got to "When will you pay it back?" She didn't need to know that. She hadn't yet gotten a satisfactory answer to "Why do you need the money?" And I want to emphasize, once again, that even if this was a game, Kyle felt she was dealing with a real ethical dilemma.

I kept wheedling, and finally I brought it up: "I'll only borrow it for a little while."

Kyle didn't bite. She didn't even ask, "How long?"

We were amazed, but she was sticking to her principles. She had to be satisfied that Janie needed the money before the discussion could go further.

Finally I said, "I won't be your friend anymore."

Kyle was hurt, but in a way she was relieved. The situation had clarified itself.

"That's your choice," she said.

Tad played Kim, a girl from a poorer family, with three younger sisters.

"Kyle, can you loan me fifty bucks? I could really use it—but if you can't loan it to me, I'll understand."

"What's it for?"

"There's this really cool denim jacket. . . ."

"Why can't you save up for it?" (Not "Why not use your own money?" this time—she was aware that Kim probably didn't have the cash on hand.)

"It's a Woodstock '94 Festival jacket. They're only selling them for a short time. If I don't buy it now, there won't be any later on."

"When can you pay it back?"

"I don't know. When will you need it? I could probably pay you, like, three dollars a week. . . ."

"No, I'll tell you what. Pay me back next February 3. That's my birthday, so we'll both remember. That's seven months from now, so you'll have plenty of time to save it up. And pay it all back at once—if you just give me a few dollars here or there, I'll just put it in my quick change and spend it. And if you don't pay it back on time . . . well . . . I'll still be your friend. But I won't ever loan you money again."

We asked her, "What if it was a friend who wanted to borrow the money to buy drugs?"

Kyle didn't hesitate. "I'll take all the money out of my medium-term savings, and I won't loan it to you, I'll *give* it to you to get into a drug treatment program. I'll go with you. But I won't loan you any money for drugs."

Later that same day, Rhett, who had overheard part of the role-playing game, came to me and made a confession. There was a bracelet he had really wanted, and a girl in school made them. She said she'd make him one for three dollars, but she needed the money in advance. Rhett gave her three dollars out of quick change, but she never made him the bracelet. What could he do?

"What did you do?"

"I asked her a whole bunch of times to keep her end of the deal and make me the bracelet, but she never did."

"What did you do next?"

"Well, then school ended, so there wasn't much more I could do . . . but what should I do now? I guess I could call her at home."

"What more can you say to her?"

"I could ask her to give me back the money if she's not going to make the bracelet. But what if she doesn't?"

"Well, what?"

"I guess I'm out three dollars."

"I guess so." I felt sad, of course—but proud. He was handling the situation responsibly. And three dollars isn't an awful lot to pay for an important life skills lesson. "What could you do differently next time?"

"I wouldn't pay her in advance. But . . . she said she had to have the money to buy the materials."

"Oh, I see. Is there any way you could deal with that?"

"Yes!" His face brightened. "I could pay her half in advance and half when I got the bracelet. Then if she didn't make it for me, I'd only be out a dollar and a half."

I've set up a structure for borrowing money within the family, and I don't believe you should encourage your school-age kids to borrow outside that structure. But there are some times in life when you may have to borrow money, and it's important that your child know that this is not a bad or shameful thing—as long as he creates a situation that both he and the friend he's borrowing from can be comfortable with. That means he has to make it clear how much he wants to borrow, when he's going to pay it back, and, if it's appropriate, what he wants to borrow the money for.

Verbal Contracts

A verbal contract is binding if it really *is* a verbal contract: if both sides understand the terms and both sides agree to them.

Kids tend to think an enforceable verbal contract can be created unilaterally, by one person saying something first, like, "Front seat!"

In a kid's world, to some extent this is true. In their own social structure—a family, a play group, a schoolyard group—kids create certain understood contracts, and one of them frequently is that whoever calls something first has first rights in a situation.

But this system works only up to a point, as every parent knows who's seen a sudden escalation to violence from two siblings arguing over who called, "Front seat!" first. A real understanding of verbal contracts is a good thing to instill early in a child.

It's not really a verbal contract if just one person says it is. "No backsies" is something you hear on the playground a lot, and it means something like this. One child has proposed a trade. The other child isn't so sure. The first child grabs the object she wants out of the second child's hand, thrusts the object she wants to trade into his hand, and calls out, "No backsies!" meaning the deal has been consummated, and you can't give it back.

A lot of schoolyard sayings promote unfairness, and while you're not going to wipe out unfairness in the schoolyard, you can at least make sure your child understands the difference, and you can teach her to be sure that she's not unfair.

"Finders keepers, losers weepers" is one of the classic examples. "Finders keepers, losers weepers" is not an inflexible rule of life: it's a justification for keeping something that doesn't belong to you, and keeping something that doesn't belong to you is stealing.

"No backsies," incidentally, can also be used in a game of tag. In this context it means if Matt tags Rachel, Rachel can't tag Matt right back— she has to go after someone else first. Or does it mean she has to go after someone else, period—she can never tag Matt back as long she's "it"? Or does it mean she has to count to three to give him a head start before she can chase him?

If the kids aren't sure, that's fertile ground for trouble. Day care provider Sue Walker says, "As soon as a fight starts to break out when my kids are playing a game, I have them sit down and talk out all the rules. They can't go back to playing until they've agreed on all of them. This is one of the first lessons I give them in negotiating a verbal contract."

Kids have to understand, as well, that a financial contract ought to be just that. It should not be used to curry favor or to lord it over a friend.

Trading

Kids will trade with each other or buy and sell anything from toys to school lunches. In this, they're in a long tradition dating back to antiquity. Barter, and the marketplace, are the cornerstones of civilization.

Your job here is to make sure your kids are trading with a knowledge of the value of things. Their first trading will be according to their own ideas of what things are worth, which may be skewed from the book value of those same things.

In other words, they may get stung.

Sydny Miner, my editor on this project, contributed a story of her seven-year-old returning from school, proudly brandishing the $3 just gotten for his new Mighty Max (list price approximately $9).

What do you do? Well, Sydny did the right thing. You can't go back to school with your child, confront the other child, and demand restitution. Basically, a deal is a deal, and if your child gets the worst of it, let it be a learning experience. Parents should not intervene in these cases.

What they can do is what Sydny did. She took her son down to the toy store and showed him what a Mighty Max costs and what kinds of toys were in the price range of his $3.

This, of course, assumes a more or less level playing field. If your children are the victims of schoolyard extortion, or severely age-inappropriate bullying, then the parents should step in.

All these borrowing and lending and trading issues may just be part of children establishing their own social structure, but they can get out

of hand, too. If your child is loaning money—and not getting it back—
to buy popularity, this is a real problem, going deeper than money, and
you need to deal with it as more than just a financial issue. You'll need
to talk seriously with your child about a range of issues relating to self-
esteem and self-worth.

Giving and Receiving

Gift Giving

Fair exchange is at the heart of most of the financial life skills lessons I've discussed in this book. That's not quite true in the case of gift giving and receiving. This is an area where the heart comes first.

But there's still plenty of room for the head to operate in the service of the heart. There are rules and guidelines that can eliminate confusion, frustration, and uncertainty and make the giving and receiving of gifts the experience of sharing from the heart that it was meant to be.

First, plan in advance. Make sure that everyone in the family has a gift-planning calendar.

Of course, you know the dates of Chanukah or Christmas or Kwanzaa or any other holiday on which your family traditionally exchanges gifts, so these will be easy to mark.

Next, mark birthdays, anniversaries, graduations, or any other special events that will require a gift.

But that's just the start of it. Knowing when a birthday is coming up is one thing . . . but when's the right time to start saving for it?

This should be marked on everyone's calendar, too—or the desktop organizer on the family computer, with a little bell programmed to go off on key days.

Make sure your kids understand the importance of giving appropriately. An overgenerous gift can indicate too much of a need for approval or control, it can embarrass the receiver, or it can signal the beginning of an unhealthy materialistic competition. Make sure your kids remember that in all situations, financial responsibility is about fairness in financial dealings as a key to fairness in all dealings.

A family meeting is a good place to set a limit on spending for each other. The limit can be a function of age—the older children, who have more, can have a larger budget, if that works for your family.

It may not. The younger children may feel hurt that they can't buy something as nice for Mom or Grandpa, and if that's the case, there are ways around it.

You can explain to kids that parents and grandparents love all gifts the same, no matter how much is spent for them. (And you can explain to your older kids, if they're lording it over their younger siblings, that they've found a good way to kill the spirit of giving, and they'd better cut it out.)

If this is really a problem, you can consider subsidizing the younger kids. Set a spending limit for all the kids based on the allowance of the oldest and make up the difference for the younger ones. This is a lesson that ought to sink in fast, and you shouldn't have to do it more than once.

A better solution is to have the kids pool their resources for one gift, with everyone putting in what he or she can afford as a percentage of their allowance.

Once your child knows how much she's going to be spending on gifts, she can begin to make a saving schedule. If she takes the cost of the gift and divides it by the amount she's going to be spending each week, then she knows how many weeks she's going to have to save, and she can mark on the calendar the week she's supposed to start saving.

For very important gift recipients within the family—perhaps parents or grandparents—you may want to help your kids get that very special gift. They should still work for each gift they're giving. But you can help them with a *matching fund*. In other words, if they save diligently according to the schedule you've agreed upon, you'll match the total.

Do this if you can afford it; don't do it if you can't. Discuss what gifts can be subsidized with a matching fund in a family meeting.

Gift giving is mostly about thoughtfulness. A gift says "I care." "I care" doesn't come through most eloquently if a gift costs more, it comes through most eloquently by how much thought has gone into the gift.

In this regard, a good game for your children is "the Christmas detective." When your child goes to visit Grandma and Grandpa, or a favorite aunt or uncle, let him do a little detective work and report back on what he's discovered about what they like. Do they have favorite colors . . . do they have special collections? Does Grandma love to wear polo shirts with an alligator on the pocket? Does Grandpa wear golf caps with interesting logos on them?

Sometimes your child can take the detective work one step farther. If Grandpa has a special hobby, maybe he does all his purchasing for that hobby at one special hobby shop, and the shopkeeper might know what he particularly wants.

Or . . . perhaps better yet . . . she can take the detective work in a different direction. Suppose she's noticed that Grandma and Grandpa have a beautiful collection of antique brass candlesticks. She isn't going to be able to afford to buy them another brass candlestick; they may not even want another. But she can polish the ones they have.

You don't have to spend money on every gift. In fact, you shouldn't. Some gifts should always be nonmonetary—it helps strike a balance. And within the family, "gift chits" for behavior or service can be the most thoughtful, the best gifts of all.

"The Christmas detective" can report in to you, and you can discuss the case. Does Grandpa have a nice garden, and does he spend all his time puttering around in it? Then he may not need a gift chit for weeding—his time in the garden may be his greatest pleasure. But if he likes the garden more than the weeding, this might be just the thing for him.

Does Grandma live in the city, six blocks from the grocery store? A week of delivery service might be just the thing for her.

Here are a couple of useful charts for gift planning:

The Gift Budget Chart

Occasion	Date	Name	Gift	$ for Gift (or chit)	Weeks to event	$ per week	OK	Match

Gift chits can be geared to the recipient's interests: for the golfer, cleaning his golf balls; for the vegetarian, cooking a gourmet vegetarian meal; for the record collector, cleaning and cataloging his old albums (make sure he doesn't do this himself regularly); for the antique car owner, waxing his car (if he'll let anyone else touch it). For the sports fan, volunteering to go to a game with him, if you haven't bought the tickets, is probably not showing the proper Christmas spirit.

Gift chits can be for delivering groceries, for yardwork, for babysitting. One of the best ones my kids ever gave me was a "No Fighting Zone" chit. It's good for three fights, and if the kids start fighting, I can pull out my chit, and they *have* to stop. (P.S. This actually works!)

Your child will write down the *occasion* (Bar Mitzvah, anniversary, Kwanzaa, whatever), the *date* by which the money has to be raised, the *name* of the person he's giving a gift to, and the *gift* itself. (Helpful hint: Remind him to budget so that he has his gift money all saved up several weeks *before* the event, so he'll have time to shop.)

In the next column he'll write the *dollar amount of the gift*, including

---

Gift is for: _____

Date gift is to be
shopped for:*   _____

Person's interests:†   _____

Favorite colors: _____

Clothing styles:††   _____

Size:§   _____

Gift and/ or
chit ideas:**   _____

** This should be well in advance of the date the gift is to be given. In fact, if you're planning a Christmas gift that you know will be available at a discount during a midsummer sale, schedule the shopping date

---

*This should be well in advance of the date the gift is to be given. In fact, if you're planning a Christmas gift that you know will be available at a discount during a midsummer sale, schedule the shopping date then, and budget your saving accordingly.

†Examples: Skiing, doing crossword puzzles, knitting, golf, reading mystery novels, antique cars, eating vegetarian food, replacing her collection of Beatle albums with CDs, following a favorite sports team.

‡Examples: Casual, bright colors, preppy, funny T-shirts, ties (plain or colorful), hippie tie-dye.

§If it's your sister Gladys, you probably know her size, and your kids can ask you. Otherwise they'll probably have to ask the recipient in person—in which case they'll have to explain why they're doing it.

**Gifts can be a golf shirt, a CD (look through the person's collection: if Grandma has three Pearl Jam albums, she'll probably appreciate the new one; otherwise probably not. If Uncle Bill has four Thelonious Monk albums, a Thelonious Monk album that he doesn't have is bound to be a hit), a book on antique cars, tickets to a game. Incidentally, store clerks can be very helpful here. "The last three books she bought were by Robert Ludlum and John Grisham; what can you recommend that she might like?"

tax, or "chit" if you're giving a gift chit. For the important people on his list—parents, grandparents—there should always be at least one gift chit.

Then he'll write in the *number of weeks to the event*, divide the dollar amount by the number of weeks, and write down that figure as *dollars per week*.

He can check the *OK* box when he's finished all his saving, and then you can check the last box when—assuming he's kept his part of the deal—you give him his *matching funds*.

Here are a few other gift-giving tips:

Pooling ideas (and/or money): With all this organization, with all your gift detective charts and planning, what if two kids decide to give Aunt Sue and Uncle Larry tickets to a Pistons game, or three kids decide to get Grandma that new Pearl Jam album she's dying for? This is fertile ground for fighting (and you might not have a valid No Fighting Zone chit). Alternatively, it can be worked out in a family meeting. Why don't the two kids pool their resources and get Aunt Sue and Uncle Larry really good seats? Why don't the three kids sit down and brainstorm about what other music Grandma likes and then apportion out one CD each? If they can't decide which one will give which, they can package all three together and give them as one group gift. A compromise is always possible if you discuss it.

Parents' letters to Santa: Why not? Why should kids have all the fun? Seriously, a list is as useful to them as it is to you. If you're like most parents, you say, "Oh, I can't think of a thing." But it's useful to your kids, and it's useful to the family dynamic.

Tad remembers one childhood Christmas when his mother announced to the family that she wanted seamless stretch nylon stockings for Christmas. Tad isn't sure he knew what seamless stretch nylon stockings were back then (he isn't sure he knows what seamless stretch nylon stockings are now), but he remembers vividly the satisfaction of actually knowing there was something he could get for his mother that she wanted.

Holidays on a budget: Kids don't automatically choose to put themselves on a budget. I talked in an earlier chapter about letting kids make a Christmas list, then taking them around to the stores so they can put a price on everything they want, then adding it up so they can see just how much they're asking for. I did this with my Oprah family, and it was one of their best lessons. The kids absolutely had no idea how much they were asking for.

I gave them the assignment of coming up with a budgetary figure for everyone in the family. Then the kids had to pare down their list to fit within the budget; they had to negotiate with each other to share expensive gifts.

If there are too many kids and not enough budget for the kids to buy for each other—either siblings or cousins—they can do a *secret Santa*. It works like this:

Every child's name is put into a hat. Each child draws a name and is responsible for buying a present—with a preagreed monetary value—for that child.

Charity

The jar system includes a jar for charity—10 percent of your child's income.

This is important. You want it to become, ultimately, a natural part of every one of your child's earning transactions. You want it to become second nature. At the same time, you want it to make them think—to remind them that there is always room in the budget to share with others. If your child has a tendency toward miserliness, which can happen, an awareness of the importance of charity helps to balance that out.

Researching different charities encourages social awareness. It can either be a family project or a project for the child to take on by herself and then report on to the family.

As with gift giving, it's important to remember that charity is more than just giving money. You should encourage your children to give of themselves as well, doing volunteer work.

There's always plenty of work to do, from trick or treating for UNICEF for the littlest ones to working as a candy striper in a hospital for a teenager. As a high school senior, Tad's stepson Dustin volunteered his time for a variety of causes. He prepared and delivered meals for Angel Food East, an organization that brought hot meals to bedridden AIDS patients. He volunteered as a teacher's aid for first-graders in his local school district. He volunteered his time at Opus 40. And he was a member of the board of directors of Sunshine for HIV Kids, an organization dedicated to helping children born with the HIV virus.

Receiving

Your child has to know that if it's the thought that counts with the gifts he gives to Grandma, it's *really* the thought that counts with the gifts she gives to him.

One generation can't always be in tune with another, and lots of times grandparents are going to give children toys that would have been appropriate when they were three years younger or clothes that could have potentially devastating repercussions for the child's social life.

For that matter, even members of the same generation don't always understand each other. A child can get an unwanted present from a friend who's just fallen madly in love with Michael Bolton and assumes everyone else should feel the same way.

What's the right way for a kid to respond to getting a present he doesn't like? Is it lying to pretend to like it?

No.

No one has a right to expect people to please them. It really *is* the thought that counts.

In any case, "This is great! Thanks a lot" is not a lie. It's great that someone thought of you.

So what should your child do with a gift she hates? If the giver of the gift says "Feel free to exchange this if you already have one," it's okay to do just that. If not . . . some people favor "recycling" it by giving it to someone else, but I believe that's a no-no. How would you feel if you went to a birthday party and saw a present you had given with love, or at least friendship, wrapped up again and given to someone else?

Things shouldn't go to waste, though. Giving it to charity is okay.

Don't forget that holidays are stressful times, especially for little children, and gracious receiving is not a natural response, it's a learned response. If your young child bursts into tears when he gets a gift he doesn't want, understand what he's going through and don't punish him for it. Instead, use it as an occasion to explain to him that it's all right to be disappointed, but you have to consider the feelings of the person who gave it to you.

Here's another message you can give your child at the same time: "Isn't it wonderful that you work and earn your own money, so that you can buy exactly what you want for yourself?" Too many kids are economically powerless—they're at the mercy of others, not just for their needs, but for all the things they want. Imagine how that must feel. If they get too much, they're spoiled; if they don't get enough, they're deprived. Either way, they're not doing for themselves. This is another little lesson in empowerment, and we can never have too many of those.

Thank-you notes are important: they are an essential part of giving time and giving of yourself. And thank-you notes shouldn't be generic. Make sure your child personalizes them and makes a specific mention of the gift he's been given.

Getting Too Much

One thing almost all parents share in common is a certain amount of shock at the number of gifts our kids receive. Many of us have experienced a Christmas or birthday turned into a feeding frenzy, with kids in a hypnotic trance, ripping open one present after another, barely able to distinguish one from another, and finally looking up with glazed eyes to mumble, "You mean that's all there is?"

Every year we vow, "This is the last time," but we don't necessarily know how to stop the merry-go-round.

We all have to learn to kick that habit. My Oprah families did. They had the courage, in the first place, to hold themselves up to the ridicule of millions of Americans who watched them, saying, "I would never let things get so out of hand." And they had the determination to do something many people never do: change their bad habits.

But what they learned, we can all learn:

1. The more your kids learn about what it means to take a responsible attitude toward money, and how they can be a part of it, the more they'll accept, even embrace, your responsible decisions.
2. They won't just arrive at this new attitude all by themselves.

We have to start somewhere to break the habit.

If all you're going to do is just pull the plug, it's going to be painful. Then the child gets only part of the lesson: life is unfair. Suddenly he's not getting something that he's been accustomed to getting. But if this is part of a whole system of financial responsibility, including work for pay, want vs. need, a jar for charitable donations, and family meetings where service to the community is discussed, then he's more likely to understand. He's more likely to take in stride the idea of a budgetary approach to birthdays and holidays. My Oprah family did.

Here are some suggestions for controlling the gift avalanche:

1. It's okay to tell relatives that your children have "college funds" that they take seriously, and that gifts to it will be received warmly.
2. It's okay to say, "We're giving to charity." For my fortieth birthday, I asked for donations to UNICEF in lieu of gifts. If you give a gift to UNICEF, or the National Wildlife Fund, or a hospital for crippled children in the name of the birthday child, the organization will send her a certificate of appreciation that she can be proud to have. If she takes it to school and shows it to her classmates, it could start a chain reaction.
3. It's okay to put your child's birthday on a budget. You pay your child an allowance based on his age—why not budget birthday guests? Four friends for a four-year-old, eight friends for an eight-year-old, and so on.
4. It's okay to set a dollar limit on gifts, even on the party invitations ("Please don't spend more than $5 a gift"). You'll find that other parents will appreciate this, too. (It could start a neighborhood chain reaction.)
5. You don't have to keep up with the Joneses on hiring clowns, animal acts, or face painters. Kids don't need those things. They tend to be pretty ingenious about amusing themselves.
6. Get the kids involved in planning their own parties and creating the games for them. Remember what Thoreau said about heating with wood—it warms you twice, once when you're chopping it and again when you're burning it. You don't need to buy a "pin the tail on the donkey" game when kids can probably make a better one for themselves; and that way, they have the fun of making it, too.
7. *The Penny Whistle Party Planner* and *Birthday Party Book* by Meredith Brokaw and Annie Gilbar (Fireside Books), is an excellent resource for do-it-yourself parties.
8. Don't forget—and don't forget to remind your child—that a birthday party is a celebration of her birth, that it's your way of saying how happy and proud you are that she is who she is.

Christmas

One of my Oprah families had six kids, and they went nuts at Christmas. They spent without counting the cost, and when the dust had settled, as we totaled it up later (not an easy task, because when you spend that furiously, it's hard to remember exactly what you've bought), they had spent about $500 on each child.

On their new budget, they cut down the next year to $150 per kid. I thought it was still a little high, but I was proud of them nonetheless. For the first time they knew what they were spending, and for the first time they had a ceiling.

The kids' Christmas budget project:

• Make out a wish list—anything goes.
• Go out to the stores with your kids and price each item on the list. Write down the prices and bring the list home.
• Get a calculator and total the value of the list (if this is your kids' first time doing it, they are likely to be in for a shock).

With that knowledge on the table, you're ready to discuss a Christmas budget at the next family meeting. With input from the kids, you'll all get a sense of what you can afford and what's appropriate for kids to be getting (this will vary from family to family, but no family needs to go overboard with conspicuous Christmas consumption). And now the kids are ready to restructure their list with realistic guidelines.

This may be a letdown from the bonanza they were hoping for originally, but it's a challenge to their ingenuity. They can combine wish lists, too—if they can agree to share that CD player that costs twice what each of their individual budgets would allow, that's allowed.

Receiving from Grandparents

First of all, your children's grandparents are your parents, so you don't need me to tell you that your control over them is probably limited. And it probably should be: grandparents are special. They like to give to their grandchildren, and they have a right to be indulged.

As Tad told me after returning from a visit to his two-year-old grandson, "I've figured out the whole secret of life. You go through all the junk that life, and fate, and the powers that be throw at you for the first fifty years or so, and then they make it all up to you by giving you grandchildren."

So let them do what they feel comfortable doing. Make sure your children know—before the situation arises—that cash gifts from grandparents will be divided among their jars—quick cash, the two savings jars, taxes, and charity.

Grandparents often love their grandchildren more than they understand them, or at least more than they understand exactly what a contemporary nine-year-old or twelve-year-old wants. So it's certainly all right for your children to give their grandparents a "wish list"—making sure, of course, that it's not too ambitious.

It's a good idea to talk over that wish list with the grandparents. While it's true that you don't want to stifle their natural instincts, you do want to let them know—in advance—if there are things on the list that you have house rules against—violent toys, for example, or sexist toys. If there's a breakdown in communication, and somehow that water gun in the shape of an AK-47 makes it through to under the tree, don't talk to the grandparent about it in front of the child. Save that for a later, private (and tactful) discussion.

What if one set of grandparents can afford much more expensive gifts than the other can?

This is a tough one. It means—and this is always true anyway—that you have to turn to those communication lines that we trust you've opened up, and make sure, once again, that your children understand that more money doesn't mean better, that more expensive gifts don't mean more love. I really believe that most kids respond to affection and warmth and love more than they do to gifts, anyway. If they don't, this is a subject for serious discussion.

If your parents (or in-laws) are on a tight budget, or a fixed income, and your kids are going to visit them, it's appropriate to try to make the financial burden of the visit easier.

When you call to arrange the visit, you can say, "I'm thrilled that the kids will be coming to see you—and I'd really like to help out. How about if I send twenty bucks with them for groceries?" Or, if they're close enough, "How about if I send over a roast?"

You can make sure that when your kids leave for a visit, they have their own pocket money with them so that all the onus of buying souvenirs at the ball game, for example, is not on the grandparents.

You can make sure the grandparents know that you've discussed the etiquette of being a good guest, and the kids won't expect to have a lot spent on them—that they're mostly just excited to see Grandma and Grandpa.

Receiving from Two Sets of Parents

What can be a problem with grandparents is potentially even touchier with divorced parents—what if one set can afford many more expensive gifts than the other can?

If you're the one with the greater income, try to make sure you're not doing things to show up the other household.

If you're the one with the smaller income, and the other parent chooses the ostentatious route, discuss it with your child, even though there's not much to say. You've made that commitment to be open with your child about money matters.

You have to tread a fine line here. Explain to your child that it's not a matter of who loves you more, just who can afford more, but be sure not to bad-mouth the other parent. That only hurts your child.

If your child comes to visit you on the weekend dressed in rags, and you decide to buy her new clothes, that's *your* decision. Try not to resent it, and don't pull your kids into whatever resentment you may feel.

A divorced-remarried household may not only create two sets of parents, it can also establish two sets of kids within the same household, or even three: yours, mine, and ours. This can take time and serious effort before everyone makes the adjustment, but it has to be done. Concentrate on fairness, and concentrate on communication.

Citizen of the Community

I believe that my most important goal in this book is to empower parents to empower their children: to give kids both the skills and the values to interact with the rest of the world. I believe that learning the skills of negotiation for fair exchange of material value can lay the groundwork for another kind of empowerment: fair exchange with the world at large in terms of respect.

Every interaction of respect is important, and every interaction is mutual. Kids today talk a lot about being "dissed"—that is, treated with disrespect. No one, child or adult, should accept being treated with disrespect. But the best way to set up an interaction based on respect is to initiate it.

Take a small but significant example: littering. If you litter, you're showing disrespect for your neighborhood, your community, your environment. If you pick up litter, you're showing respect. In either case, there's likely to be a chain reaction. Litter attracts litter. People are more likely to just toss something aside in an area that's already littered than they are in an area that's neat. In just the same way, picking up can attract picking up.

I believe that this is an area where our society is improving. When I was younger, most people really didn't think environmentally. You might toss a candy wrapper out of the window of your car, or a soda can over the side of your boat, without thinking twice. Now, many more people are aware of how destructive that is.

Ethics

It's never too early to start your children thinking about ethical behavior. This can be another good source of games for the car, where you're all together and it's easy for conversation to flow back and forth.

For little ones, you can write good and bad behavior traits on pieces of paper and put them in a *behavior bag.* Here are some examples:

Good   **Bad**

Nice to others   Dishonest
Fair   Unfair
Honest   Cheater
Loyal   Mean
Trustworthy   Dangerous

Each child draws a paper out of the bag, reads what's written on it, and says whether it's good or bad. Then everyone has to give an example of that kind of behavior, from real life or from a hypothetical situation or even from fiction—a favorite book or movie.

You can also have an *ethical decision bag.* This is a little different—the slips of paper here contain situations, and the question everyone has to answer is, What would you do . . .

- if you saw a wallet lying in the bushes?
- if someone gave you too much change?
- if your teacher wasn't watching, and the person at the desk next to you knew all the answers to the test?
- if you went to buy a newspaper from a machine, and the door hadn't clicked shut all the way?
- if you were visiting a friend and he'd left some money out on his dresser? Would he mind if you "borrowed" it?
- if your teacher wasn't watching, and the person in front of you read the answers off someone else's paper?
- if your best friend told you a secret and made you promise not to tell?
- if a friend told you a secret about someone else, and you were pretty sure that the other person wouldn't want it to have been told?
- if your sister or brother got blamed for something you'd done?
- if your older sister or brother was alone with her/his steady, and they didn't know you could hear them?

- if something you really wanted was lying on the counter of a store, and there was no one around?

I'm sure you can come up with more.

Value Judgments

Value can be a concrete expression of how much something is *actually worth* in terms of money or any other concrete measure of exchange like barter. But value can also refer to a *value judgment*, which means *your opinion* of how much something is worth. This isn't concrete, it's purely personal, and one person's answer is as good as another's.

To play the value judgment game in the car, prepare a bag full of little sayings. One child can draw a saying out of the bag, and then everyone can give an opinion, on a scale of one to ten, of how much they agree with the saying. Here are a few examples:

> Chocolate-chip cookies are great.
> TV is more fun than doing homework.
> Everything always turns out for the best.
> Children should be seen and not heard.
> Strawberry yogurt tastes terrible.
> Tall people should play basketball.
> Girls are smarter than boys.
> The Knicks are better than the Lakers.

Most statements are opinions and not facts. It's important that your kids learn the distinction.

Bringing the Community into Family Meetings

The family meeting is one of your important interfaces between your home and the world at large, so it's not a bad idea to devote some time at these meetings to community issues. These can include:

Community service issues, like charities. Here's where you discuss what charities your family wants to get involved with. You can talk about different charities: what they do and how well they do what they do.

One of the best charities for little children is UNICEF, because it's kids giving for kids. The annual Halloween Trick or Treat for UNICEF is fun, and it's part of the festive Halloween spirit. But what does it actually mean? What does UNICEF do?* At a family meeting, you can explain this, and other family members can make presentations for their favorite charities. Suppose, for instance, your teenager has started playing in a band, she's discovered the great legacy of American music created by artists who never got paid for what they did, and she wants the family to support the Rhythm and Blues Foundation. She can make her case for it at a family meeting, and the family will give her a fair hearing and discussion.

Other charities that children may be interested in are the Make-a-Wish Foundation, Ronald McDonald House, and Sunshine for HIV Kids. And don't overlook local community charities. Charity begins at home, and your kids can see both the problem and the effect of their work when you give money and time locally.

The family should decide on the number of charities it will contribute to. One to three is generally plenty.

Do all charities actually do what they say they're doing? Do they all deliver your contributed dollar equally well? If someone in your family stays up and watches late night TV, she'll see lots of commercials for organizations that ask you to sponsor a child in a poverty-torn part of the world. Are they all equally good?

Forbes magazine regularly carries an excellent breakdown of how a number of charities slice up the money that's contributed to them—how much goes to salaries and administrative costs, how much actually is put to work helping people. You can get a lot of information on this and other consumer issues from *The Consumer Resource Handbook*, available for free from the Superintendent of Documents, Government Printing Office, Public Document Distribution Center, Pueblo, CO 81009. Your local Better Business Bureau or Chamber of Commerce can be an excellent source for information about charities.

---

*I'm particularly familiar with UNICEF as a member of the board of directors of the U.S. Committee of UNICEF. It's concerned with helping children, educating mothers, and combating preventable disease throughout the world. Over forty thousand children worldwide die of preventable diseases every day. UNICEF, through its immunization and education programs, has actually helped eradicate a number of diseases.

Community issues, like local school bond proposals, community work or cultural projects, or recycling campaigns. What are the issues? How does the family feel about it? Does the family want to get involved?

Current events. You've talked to your children about taxes and what they do in an ideal world; use this opportunity to discuss what they're doing in the real world. Civic responsibility is a natural outgrowth of financial responsibility.

Breakage

Breaking something that doesn't belong to you is a problem both inside the family and outside in the greater community. Everyone knows that it's not good to break things, and that in most cases nobody means to do it, and that in most cases the person who broke something is going to be sorry.

But in the case of breaking something an apology isn't quite enough. Restitution is needed, too.

That doesn't mean that breaking something by accident is a terrible thing. Accidents happen. Sometimes they happen through carelessness, and that should be addressed; sometimes they just happen.

In fact—and this is easier said than done—if you can restrain yourself from blowing up when something gets broken, you should try to. Yelling when something is broken tends to send a message that things are more important than people.

The reward—or punishment—for behavioral matters should be behavioral; the reward—or punishment—for material matters should be material. If you break something, you should pay for it, in time or money or both.

Not taking the breakage seriously enough sends a damaging message, too: that it's not really important to respect the boundaries of others.

I learned that lesson for myself when I was about twelve. A girlfriend and I got a couple of brushes and a couple of cans of white paint and set out to write "Ringo for President" all over the sidewalks in our neighborhood. I guess we hadn't thought it through well enough to realize that Ringo was British and therefore ineligible to be president, but that was actually the least of what we hadn't thought through. We thought we were using a water-based paint, but it turned out to be a particularly rugged sort of latex house paint.

We had thought we weren't going to get caught, but within an hour after we had run home and were giggling upstairs in my bedroom, a policeman knocked at the door.

"Are you the two girls who painted up the streets?" he asked.

We weren't cut out for a life of crime. We confessed immediately.

"But how did you catch us?" I wanted to know.

The policeman smiled and pointed behind him.

We looked.

Across the front porch, down the steps, and out along the street was the evidence: our footprints in white paint, heading straight to the door.

I paid in both community service and money. I had to scrape every last "Ringo for President" off the sidewalks with a stiff wire brush, and I had to buy my own wire brush for the job.

Your child also has to understand that if he has friends over to visit, he's responsible for his friends' behavior as well. If your child and his friends take over the family computer to play Dungeons and Dragons, and one of his friends accidentally enters a series of commands that cuts off all communication between the keyboard and the central processing unit, so that no matter how hard you bang down on the keys nothing appears on the screen, and the computer technician has to be called in, your child is responsible for picking up the tab.

You're very likely to get a chorus of "No fair!" on this rule. "Why am I responsible both ways? If I go over to someone else's house and break something, I have to pay. If someone else comes over to my house and breaks something, I have to pay."

For an answer, refer him back to "our rules": this is the way *we* do things. If his friend has also been raised to be financially responsible, he'll assume the burden. But we have no control over the rules in other households, only our own.

What happens if a child breaks something that's far beyond his ability to pay for it? That can happen, and sometimes spectacularly. I remember—and this is not a fond memory—something that happened to a friend of mine not long ago. We'll call her Denise. She owned a house in the country and fifty-six acres of farmland, and she had recently acquired a tractor (which she had just finished paying for and was the apple of her eye) and a new husband (who was, as husbands tend to be, a mixed blessing).

With her husband, she had acquired a fourteen-year-old stepson (which is truly a mixed blessing), and the stepson and a friend were visiting at the farm.

Somehow they had cajoled Denise (or her husband—memory gets fuzzy on this part of the story, though the rest is as vivid as an earthquake) into letting them try out the tractor. They promised to be careful, but the temptation to convert a piece of heavy farm machinery into a go-cart was too strong.

On the farm, in the middle of the fifty-six acres, was a little pond. If they had been aiming at it, they probably wouldn't have been able to hit it. But as fate would have it, they managed to line up the tractor so it was bearing right down on the pond, and they couldn't seem to stop it or turn it. They did manage to bail out just in time, allowing the tractor to barrel on ahead into the pond.

The damage to Denise: one ruined tractor; the cost of towing the tractor out of the pond and disposing of it; one polluted pond that had to be drained and restored by environmental professionals.

This story does not have a happy ending. Denise's stepson's mother's response was, "Gee, that sure is bad luck. Well, accidents happen." Denise never did find out what the other boy's parents felt, because they never bothered to contact her.

This was wrong. It was unfair to Denise, and it was letting the kids down, too, by sending them the wrong message. It was teaching them to be the kind of people we don't want our kids to be.

This was a leviathan of a preventable accident caused by carelessness. It was destructive of property, and it was destructive of the environment. The monetary damage was way up in the thousands—well beyond any kid's capacity to make financial restitution.

But the boys should have contributed something. They should have contributed enough money to feel the bite of it—a few hundred dollars, anyway—and they should have worked on the restoration of the pond.

Here's another story. When Rhett was five and Kyle was eight, Kyle felt it was time she had privacy in the bathroom, and we agreed. We told

Rhett that he couldn't go barging into the bathroom—or any other room with a closed door—without knocking. Rhett complained that knocking hurt his knuckles, and that kicking was a much more effective way of announcing his presence.

It turned out he was right. It was such an effective way that one morning he kicked a hole in the bottom panel of the bathroom door.

It doesn't say much for the bathroom door that a five-year-old was able to kick it in. But it was the only bathroom door we had, and Rhett was responsible for it, and it had to be replaced. (Rhett's solution, incidentally, was to decorate it: he wanted to paint a big daisy on it, with the hole as the center. That solution had to be rejected.)

This was New York City, and the cost of a new door, installed, was $300. Rhett was brought into the process of the replacement of the door. He understood what was involved in it—the work and the financial obligation—and he contributed a portion of the cost. He paid 10 percent of the total price: $30. He also had to go with me to the door store, where he saw the price of a new door, and he went with me to the handyman, who discussed the job and his estimate for doing the job. He was also in attendance when the job was done.

We haven't had to replace another door.

Shoplifting

Shoplifting is a serious matter, and the vast majority of kids do it at one time or another. Most of them do it because they don't realize exactly how serious it is. The punishment has to be financial, but it's even more important that your child feel the spotlight of social disapproval. The punishment I recommend is that the child return to store, pay for the object, and tell the shopkeeper what she's done.

Kids must also understand that pocketing too much change is stealing, that finding a wallet and not returning it is stealing, that "Finders keepers, losers weepers" is stealing.

Ethics is all about fairness, and a sense of fairness comes from self-respect, self-reliance, self-worth. Working for pay—coming to understand, in Shakespeare's words, that "nothing will come of nothing," but that you can take your life into your own hands and make something of it—all of this can contribute to building character in a child who doesn't expect a wallet to fall magically into her hands, and what's more, who understands that it *is* someone else's wallet, representing money that someone else earned fairly and that someone else has a right to.

The Smart Consumer

Here's a checklist for smart consumers:

- *Get the best buy for the best price.* Don't forget that means both of the above—getting the best price all by itself isn't enough.
- *Make sure you know the store's return policy.* Even if a store has the best prices, if it's an item you're not sure of, it's no good to you if you don't have the option of returning it. A store may also have a different return policy for sale merchandise.
- *Don't forget to keep receipts.* The best return policy in the world—. or the best warranty in the world—isn't going to help you if you can't prove when and where you bought the item.
- *Shop a season ahead.* Clothing items fluctuate a lot in price; shop out of season for the best prices.
- *Shop sales.* Ski accessories aren't going to be on sale in the winter; but if you're a skier, or someone on your gift list is a skier, you know that you'll need them eventually.
- *Know your rights.* Did you know that stores are contractually obligated to credit card companies to accept *every* charge? They can put up signs saying "No Charges on Purchases Under . . ." but they can't enforce them legally. Did you know that if you want three tomatoes out of a package of ten, the supermarket is obligated to open the package and let you take your three?
- *What's new? What's not?* Do you have to buy new? Sometimes secondhand products are just as good as new and a lot cheaper. Sometimes they're more trouble than they're worth. Do your research on this before you go shopping.

  Even if you're buying new, what about brand names? Are off brands, or store brands, as good as the major names for this particular product? *Consumer Reports* does an excellent job of armchair comparison shopping for you on a whole range of products. If you don't subscribe, your library certainly has it.

- *Service.* How about service? If you're not likely to need it, a deep discount house or mail-order catalog may be your best bet. If you think you're going to want someone to handle problems or explain things you don't understand, a local store may be better, even if the initial price is higher.

Here's an example: Tad bought his laptop computer from a local merchant. Recently the modem just stopped working for what appeared to be no reason. He had two different modem programs, and neither of them worked. He had bought his computer locally and took it into the store. They found the problem—or, rather, the problems—in twenty minutes. By a strange but not unheard-of coincidence, each program had a different software error. He walked out with a working computer and no charge for the service. If he had bought it from a catalog house—well, they all have telephone technical support, and they might have been able to talk him through it over the phone. Then again, they might not have.

The World As a Classroom

The classroom—at home or at school—is designed to prepare your kids for the world, but you can also use the world itself as your classroom. It's out there, and it has any number of lessons to offer if you stay alert to them.

You don't even need to step outside your front door, as a matter of fact. The world comes into your home every day, often more than you want it to, thanks to that big unblinking eye in the middle of your living room, the TV.

There's no point in decrying the fact that TV exists, or that your kids are subject to a dizzying barrage of commercials on it. It does, and they are. So make use of it. Talk to your kids about what they see on TV.

We are the largest capitalist nation in the world. This is not something for which we have to apologize. It means we have an incredible amount of choice, which is both an advantage and a challenge. It means we have to make intelligent decisions about those choices, based on all the data we have. TV commercials are part of that data, but they're not always the most reliable data, and the information you get from them has to be evaluated carefully. The first rule of thumb here is, "If it looks too good to be true, it probably is." This is a valuable lesson to learn early, because the same thing will be true later in life when your kids start looking at investments.

For young children, this means explaining something that's obvious to you, though not necessarily obvious to them: there's a difference between programs and commercials.

This distinction is not always obvious (think about all those "infomercials"!), especially on children's Saturday morning television, where the line between programming and salesmanship is easily blurred. Marketing experts are starting to work on your child very early, trying to develop the habits of consumer loyalty. You should be working just as hard, developing the habits of consumer selectivity.

Watch a few programs with them and explain the difference: this is the part where they're telling you a story, this is the part where they're trying to talk you into going out and buying something. You can give them their first lessons about being an informed consumer: this is what they're saying on television to make you want to buy something; these are the things you need to find out before you know whether something is worth buying.

As your children get older, they can continue to develop and refine their skills of commercial watching. Discuss these questions with them: What are the advertisers trying to make you think about when you watch a commercial for this product? What are they trying to make you not think about? What should you be thinking about when you evaluate the quality and value of the product?

Those same informed consumer issues can be developed further in more want vs. need games. Applied to grocery shopping, want vs. need can teach good nutrition lessons. For example, we all need food, of course, but what kinds of food really satisfy our nutritional needs, and what kinds of food do we buy and eat just because we want it? Let kids make the comparisons between the foods they like: "fruit beverages" compared to 100 percent juice; sweetened and unsweetened fruit cereals; home-popped popcorn and the packaged variety; cheese puff snacks and real cheese and crackers.

Physical/Fiscal Fitness

I've talked about how the lessons of financial responsibility can extend to other areas of your child's life, and this is a case in point. You've studied budgeting as a family—how about the budgeting of nutrition? Here's a good research project for your child: setting up a want vs. need nutritional budget. Have him draw up a chart, similar to the budget chart, of daily nutritional needs and maximum percentage of fat to a healthy diet.

Point out to him the similarity between this chart and his financial charts—budget charts, fixed vs. variable expenses, want vs. need lists. This is another example of how a healthy attitude toward money relates to other healthy attitudes. Financial responsibility teaches fair exchange of values. A fair exchange of values in the field of nutrition means that satisfying nutritional needs, and rationing desires for sweets and junk food, equals a healthy body.

In other words, there's a definite link between fiscal fitness and physical fitness.

Time Value of Money

The smart consumer pays attention to the time value of money.

At first those questions are easy. Should you buy something little today or save it and buy something better next week? Later on they get more difficult. Should you save your money or invest it right now in raw materials for a business venture that might make you more money?

These are time value of money questions, and financial professionals wrestle with them all the time.

Money has value today. That's present value.

The same money will have a different value tomorrow. That's future value.

Here's a simple example. Say you have $100 now, and you want to buy a $100 dress. If you invest your money at an 8 percent rate of return, in six months you can still buy the dress, and you'll have $4 left over. But if it's the off season for the dress now, so it's on sale for $90, you can buy it now, invest the remaining $10, and at the end of six months you'll have the dress and $10.40.

Of course (now we're making it more complicated), you could buy the dress now, and six months from now styles could have changed, your tastes could have changed, you could have gained or lost weight so it doesn't fit anymore, and then you've got $10.40 and a dress you can't wear.

Or you could take the $100, buy twenty pieces of costume jewelry at $5 apiece, and sell them over the next six months for $7 apiece, which would give you the dress and $40 . . . *if* you sold them all.

You are trying to teach your children to use money effectively and efficiently, and getting them to understand the concept of time value of money gives them one very good tool.

The "what if" game is a good one to show your kids how to think about money. The "what if" game is very simple:

What if you had $1,000? What would you do with it?
What if you had $10,000?
What if you had $100,000?
What if you had a million dollars?

Have your child map out a plan for each sum. What would she do with it? What would she save? What would she buy? How much would she give to charity?

This game can, of course, be played over and over, and it should be. Children's sense of values change, and so does their level of financial sophistication.

Why not keep a record of your child's answers in the family journal? Then play the game again a year later and compare the results.

The Smart Consumer's Budget

You can teach your child to make up a personal budget.

The first step here is to make up a *personal expense log*. Buy your child a small, pocket-size notebook and a pen or pencil. On every page of the notebook, write the following:

```
Day of the week: _____
Amount spent: $_____
Item bought: _____
Need or want: _____
```

Have your child write down everything he spends money on all week. The only rule is, he has to make sure he writes it down as soon as he spends it, or he'll forget.

After your child keeps his log for a week, sit down and review it with him. Is his spending pattern what he thought it was, or are there any surprises? Any regrets? Talk about needs vs. wants with him and how his spending falls across the need-want continuum.

Remind your child that we all have a limited amount of money to spend, and we all have to make choices. When he starts making those choices for himself, he's entering the world of personal money management—the process of choice that influences every dollar he spends.

Remind him an awareness of need and want underlies every one of those choices. A good budget enables him to pay for what he needs and save up for what he wants.

Now get some fresh paper (or a new file on the family computer) and start making up a budget with him. Help him come up with a group of categories that will cover everything he spends money on, such as these likely possibilities:

Food
Clothing
Gifts
Entertainment
Hobbies

After everything in the notebook has been put into one category or another, go over each category and decide which items are needs and which items are wants.

Some categories will include both "need" *and* "want" items. For example, he may need a school lunch but want the ice-cream bar he buys for dessert.

Now make up a tentative budget. Budgeting is a dynamic process, with a lot of give and take. The first budget your child creates won't necessarily be the model he's still following a year later or six months later. Needs change, wants change, incomes change, spending patterns change.

Rachel's Weekly Budget

Category	Fixed Expense	$	Variable expense	$	Act. spent
Food	School lunch		After-school snack		
Entertainment			Movie		
Clothes	Save for new jeans — 10% per week		Save extra for designer jeans		
Total					

At the end of a week, and again at the end of the month, sit down with your child and compare the projected budget with what's actually being spent.

Have her ask herself these questions:

1. Did I spend more or less than I budgeted?
2. If I spent more—why? Was it "impulse" buying? Were there any unplanned expenses?
3. If I had the week to do over again, what would I change?

If she is spending more than she's budgeted for, then it's time to either cut back or adjust the budget.

Time Consumers

Time, like money, is a finite resource. There are only twenty-four hours in a day, and nobody is going to give you any more. So time has to be budgeted, too, and your kids need to be taught to be smart consumers, not spendthrifts, of time as well as money.

Just as there are fixed and variable expenses in a budget, the outlay of time can be fixed and variable, too. A good way to show your kids how this works is to have them chart how they spend their time.

First have them keep a log for a few days—weekdays and over a weekend—of everything they do and how much time they spend doing it. Then have them enter the information into a *time value chart*. The first chart they make out will be entering the time they actually spend; after that, you can work with them to create a time value chart that reflects the time budget of a smart consumer.

Here's a time value chart you can use:

Patrick's Time Value Chart

Activity	Fix	Var.	Time Spent	% of Day
School				
Sleeping				
Chores				
Odd jobs				
TV				
Homework				
Grooming				
Talking on the phone				
Sports (play and practice)				
Worship				
Hanging out with friends				

Some activities, of course, represent a fixed allocation of time up to a point; then they become negotiable. Your child needs to devote a certain amount of time to grooming, but he doesn't *need* to devote three hours a day to it.

A second useful tool is the *guilt-free time budget chart*. Just as your child has a guilt-free budget for his spending money, he can budget his own spare time after he's finished taking care of the things he has to do.

But it might be useful for him to assess—for his own benefit—how he is using that time and whether he's using it to his best advantage. He already knows, from his time value chart, how much time he's spending on various activities. In this chart he gets to evaluate it.

Patrick's Guilt-Free Time Budget
Chart (____hours free time)

Activity	Time	% of Time	Value 1–10	Value
Hanging out with friends				
Sports (play and practice)				
Music Lessons and practice				
Video/computer games				
Hiking				
Camping				
Daydreaming				
Reading				

After logging in the activity, the time spent on it, and the percentage that represents of his total free time, your child should put a value on how meaningful that activity is to him, using a scale of one to ten. How would he describe the value of the activity?

Your child is not answerable to anyone but himself here. This is his own time, his own guilt-free time budget. But it can make for a good self-assessment and perhaps some reevaluation.

Career Development

Your child doesn't have to declare a career in grade school, or junior high, or even in high school. And there's nothing wrong with the child who comes up every week with a new ambition for what she wants to do when she grows up. It shows a healthy, inquiring mind.

But there are some guidelines you can use to get a sense of where your child is heading. Your ultimate goal, of course, is to open up a path that will lead your child to a career and a way of life that she'll be happy with.

If you know what kind of general orientation your child has, it can be helpful when you talk to her about her future, either playing-around talk when she's little or more serious talk as she gets older.

Remember, none of this is set in stone. It's all an exercise to help your children discover who they are and who and what they want to become.

Career development games and exercises for a school-age child are a process, not a means to an end.

The same is true of education. Think of education as an attitude, not just an acquisition. Education is a continuum, a lifelong process of growth and self-examination. Think of this "career development" chapter as just a part of that continuum.

Mr. Potato Head

This is a game I've played with kids of all ages, even those who are too old to sit down and play with Mr. Potato Head by choice.

I start with the Mr. Potato Head game. I put all the different pieces in different boxes—the eyes in one, the ears in another—and label the boxes.

The eyes are *Vision: attention to detail.*
The ears are *Attentiveness: sensitivity to what's around you, inter-est in what others have to say.*
The mouth is *Persuasiveness: the ability to communicate.*
The nose is *Sensitivity to tastes and aromas,* or it can be *Inquisi-tiveness,* or *Common sense: the ability to see what's under your nose.*
The hands are *Aptitude for work: the skills of a craftsperson.*
The feet can be *Someone who's well grounded,* or *Someone who likes to travel.*

Put all together, these different characteristics coalesce into one whole person, one Mr. or Ms. Potato Head. This is a good game for kids, because they often tend to pigeonhole themselves or accept the pigeonholing that adults give them ("I'm no good at math," "I'm just naturally shy"). But all these different skills, or interests, or personality types, can come together.

Play the game again, letting the kids come up with labels for each of the boxes. See what characteristics they come up with.

Who Am I?

Here's a worksheet for your child to start taking stock of himself. This activity is more self-conscious than the Mr. Potato Head —your child will have to think about who he is, instead of revealing himself through instinctive behavior.

Name _____

My favorite things to do are _____

_____

_____

_____

I (like, don't like) to use computers _____

I like to play (team, individual) sports _____

I hate to _____

I'm afraid of _____

I (like, don't like) to read _____

I (like, don't like) to talk to people _____

Entrepreneurship

Is your child likely to be an entrepreneur or a wage earner? Many of us have a little of both in our personalities, and we may move from one to the other at different times in our lives. I went from working in a bank to running my own small business, the Children's Financial Network.

A wage earner is happiest with the security of a regular paycheck, the solidity of a structured work environment. An entrepreneur is willing to give up that security for the satisfaction of being her own boss.

Not everyone is cut out to be an entrepreneur. It's a good idea to try it out as a kid, when the stakes are smaller, to find out.

Entrepreneur training programs are available at all grade levels. I'm currently working with three of them: One to One, Junior Achievement, and the Salvation Army.

Lots of states also sponsor programs for kids to learn about business. To locate programs in your state, write:

The National Council on Economic Education
1140 Avenue of the Americas
New York, NY 10036
Phone (212) 730-7007

Resources and educational opportunities for future entrepreneurs are also available from:

The Center for Entrepreneurship
Wichita State University
1845 North Fairmount
Wichita, KS 67260
Phone (316) 689-3000

Your Work and Your Kids

Let your children see what you do during your workday. If you can, bring them into your workplace and explain what your responsibilities are. Kids understand things they can see. They make concrete connections—especially younger children. If you're a butcher or a pilot, they can understand that; if you work in an office, it's not so clear unless you take the time to make it clear.

Kids make sense of things in terms of what they know, and they try to fit what they don't know into terms that'll make sense to them. When Kyle was little and I was still president of The First Women's Bank, I was hospitalized for an extended stay because of complications in my pregnancy with Rhett. I had to carry out a lot of business from my hospital bed. Practicing what I preached, I had Kyle visit me and talked to her about what I was doing, but for a while she got the idea that the hospital room *was* my office.

If your work is taking care of a home and children, make sure that your own children understand the nature—and the economic importance—of that work. And make sure they understand how it works, too: how many business and managerial skills go into making a home, as well as craft skills like cooking and the maintenance skills needed for small (or sometimes large) repair jobs.

Just as kids notice that people live in different kinds of houses, dress differently, have bigger or smaller cars and more or fewer things, they're going to notice that jobs have different salaries. It's important to explain to kids that different types of jobs pay different salaries and to explain how and why that happens: that different types of jobs need different levels and kinds of education, and that while this makes some difference in compensation, ultimately it's the marketplace that determines how much someone makes. Talk to your kids about job satisfaction, and make sure they understand that value of job and salary are not necessarily related.

Watch Those Messages You're Sending!

Language is a powerful tool, and it's one that is always at work. If we're not conscious of the messages we're sending, then we're sending unconscious messages, but they're being received just the same.

I've talked about this earlier: the unconscious messages we send our kids about taxes, for example. Unless you're a libertarian, you know that taxes serve at least some useful purposes. But it's very easy to send the opposite message to kids without even realizing it.

Need vs. want messages are particularly easy ground for careless language. Consider the following:

"You don't need another toy." As opposed to those times when you do need a toy? Toys are never needs. And there's no point saying, "You don't want another toy," because that's almost certainly not true. If you have a "thing limit," a limit on the number of nonneeded possessions your kid can acquire over a certain time span, then "You can't have another toy" is appropriate. It may sound meaner than you want to sound, but it's the house rule. Otherwise, it's your child's quick cash, and he can buy the toy whether he needs it or not (which, of course, he doesn't).

"Oh, I feel so blue today—I really need a hot-fudge sundae." Don't start telling me about endorphins—you don't *need* the sundae.

Kids first learn about the outside world from their parents, and they're not always going to be able to distinguish hyperbole from straight reporting. Griping about taxes is only one example. Here are some others:

"I hate my boss." I'm not saying this can't be true. But it very often isn't; it's just a colorful response to some specific problem in the workplace. However, if little ears pick it up, it may have the effect of encouraging disrespect for authority.

That's not good, and neither is mindless obedience to authority. If there's a problem with the boss, it's appropriate to talk about the problem and what you can do to remedy it. Kids can learn a valuable lesson from the example of a parent standing up for her rights.

How often have you come home from a difficult day on the job and said, "I hate work!"

Again, you might want to bite your tongue or at least go on to explain that you don't mean it literally. You don't want to encourage shirking or a lack of respect for the value of an honest day's work. On the other hand, it's all right to let kids know that not every day at work—or school—is going to be wonderful.

Generation Gap Anger

Sometimes it's hard to remember that we were young once. Sometimes it's even harder to remember that we're not young anymore, and that things have changed since we were.

Things do cost more today. "You paid *what* for a pair of sneakers?" sends a message to your child that you don't think much of her judgment, and you think she's some dumb cluck who allows herself to get taken. Sneakers cost a lot more than they used to. They're also a different product from what they used to be. It's almost like having your father say, "You paid *what* for a portable typewriter?" when what you really bought was a laptop computer.

It is really easy to get mad at kids for being kids. We're all human. But those aren't really your whole feelings, even your principal feelings, about your children, and it's not helpful to vent them. Of course you're going to do it sometimes—everyone has to blow off steam. But when you get right down to it, what kind of a message is, "You stupid kids! How could you not have known better than to play ball near the window"? What kind of a message is, "You're a bad boy! Only bad boys leave their toys around"?

Punishment is the consequence for inappropriate behavior—not to exact revenge on kids or to teach them that they're stupid or bad. The punishment for misbehaving or breaking the house rules is a loss of privileges. The punishment for breaking property is money and time: money to pay, or help pay, for fixing it, time to be to some degree involved in the process of fixing it. The punishment for not doing something is to do it—it teaches a time value of time lesson.

Dodging the Truth

We put ourselves in danger of crossing the line to lying every time we say, "We'll see," when we don't really mean it.

If you know that you're going to say, "No," don't put it off till later. Say it now.

"We'll see" can be appropriate *if* you really mean it; that is, if the situation has to be analyzed before you can make a decision. If this is really the case, explain to your child what you need to consider, and include your child in the decision-making process as much as possible.

"We can't afford it" can have the same effect. When you say, "We can't afford it," and it's something you actually can afford, it may scare your child about the family financial situation. Or he may conclude that you aren't telling him the truth. If you really can't afford it, make sure your child understands why it doesn't fit into your family budget.

If you're considering a large purchase, like a house or a car, you may need to study your options to decide whether you can afford it and what you can afford. This is legitimate—and it's one case where "We'll see," explained properly, is okay.

If it's a question of something you believe would be inappropriate to spend a lot of money on, you can say that. If you simply don't choose to allocate the family budget to include this particular purchase, you can say that, too: It is *absolutely* acceptable.

Keeping Your Word

The Galápagos Islands are one of the most romantic—and educational—places I can imagine in the world. To take my children to where Charles Darwin formulated his theories, to see those giant tortoises and all the other wonderful creatures that still roam wild there, is one of our family's dreams.

When *Money Doesn't Grow on Trees* was published, I said to Rhett (in the spirit of what I assumed was totally unwarranted enthusiasm), "When my book gets to number one on the *Times* best-seller list, we'll be able to go to the Galápagos Islands."

I said it and promptly forgot about it. Eight months later, to my disbelief and delight, *Money Doesn't Grow on Trees* went to number one on *The New York Times Book Review* best-seller list.

When we heard the news, we whooped with joy. "We've got to start planning a party," I said.

"And we've got to start planning our trip to the Galápagos," Rhett said.

I didn't remember. He remembered. And he'd been waiting patiently.

I thought about the time when I was ten years old and I wanted a lion. I asked my father.

"It's not so easy to get a lion as you might think," he told me.

I said, "I bet I could get one."

"All right," he said, "if you can get your own lion, you can keep it." I don't remember if he patted me on the head or not.

Well, he was right. It's not all that easy to get a lion.

It took me six months.

I corresponded with the Bronx Zoo. I told them the important stuff, which was what I needed to know, and left out the unimportant stuff, like my age. They were very helpful. They told me that first you needed to put in an order with a licensed safari, and they gave me some names and addresses. I sent out a bunch of letters, found a safari that was just being organized, and gave them my order. A lion cub cost $500 back in 1961, but even at age ten I'd been working and saving money, so I could pay them the $500 in advance without having to go to my parents and put up with a lot of bothersome questions.

The rest was all a matter of navigating through the red tape. I had to arrange for him to be quarantined for a certain number of weeks at the zoo. I researched the town ordinance on keeping wild animals, and I found that you could actually keep a lion as long as he had his shots, was declawed, and had his eyeteeth removed. Oh, and he had to be neutered at two years old. I'm not sure I exactly understood what that was, but I had a general idea.

I arranged with the zoo vet to have all that taken care of, and I got my license from the town. Then one day I went up to my father and told him, "My lion arrives on Tuesday, and we have to go to the Bronx Zoo and check him in."

He didn't let me keep it. And no, I don't believe I'd let my kids have a lion, either. But I hope I never promise my kids something I can't deliver, either.

We're budgeting right now for a trip to the Galápagos Islands. I think we'll make it in the next couple of years. Rhett's not quite so optimistic, but he's definitely counting on seeing the Galápagos sometime in the next forty years.

Part Three
Teenagers

Smooth and Painless?

The teenage years are the dress rehearsal for real life. In fact, they're more than the dress rehearsal, they're the preview performances.

If all the world's a stage, your teenager is getting ready for the role of his life—that of himself as a mature adult. He's reading his lines "off the book" now; he's in costume; he's formed the motivation for his character.

He can still make mistakes and correct them. But he's gotten to the point where he can also make serious mistakes that can't be corrected.

His next stop is the big time, the real world. This is the last chance to learn what he still doesn't know in a relatively safe environment.

The importance of the teenage years, then, is that last-minute coaching, the last pieces of information your young adult will need before she moves away from home and becomes a full-fledged adult. Your important job is making that eventual movement away from home as smooth and painless as possible.

If your teenager, or about-to-be teenager, has absorbed all the lessons and techniques in the earlier chapters of this book, it's time to move on to this section.

But if you're just now buying this book, and your children are already in their teens or close to it, much of the earlier advice—the jar system, family meetings, family banking, household citizenship—can still be useful. Those techniques don't apply only to young children, and there's nothing wrong with going back and starting them with your teenager.

Many of you who have teenagers, or have been teenagers, or have ever seen teenagers, are going to be questioning right about now how the words *smooth and painless* fit into a teenage chapter. And of course, no system can guarantee this or even come close. The teenage years begin with a universe in which parents are gods and end with a universe in which parents are those nice old folks you visit for Thanksgiving. This has to be a cataclysmic shift—for you even more than for your kids, because you're losing such an eminent position and because it is accomplished over a period of time in which your kids never doubt for a second that they're right and you're wrong.

It starts earlier than you want it to and ends later than you want it to. I tried to ease into it gently with Kyle, not quite a teenager yet. "Darling," I told her, "I just want you to know that soon there'll come a time when Mom will seem like the stupidest person in the world to you; but then when you're in your early twenties, I'll somehow miraculously grow smart again."

Kyle patted my hand. "Don't worry, Mom," she said. "I already think you're the stupidest person in the world."

We all remember (at least partially) what it was like to be a teenager. The memories are impressionistic, but vivid. I remember spending hours teasing my hair, taping my bangs, ironing my hair straight (and once being taken to the emergency room with an iron burn on my neck). I remember coming downstairs one day looking *fab*—ironed hair, white lipstick, white nail polish, black eyeliner, skirt rolled up so that it ended two-thirds of the way up my thighs, huge mohair sweater—and hearing my father say, as I hit the bottom step, "You look like a trollop."

I was furious. Not only did I know that he didn't *understand,* I knew something even worse: I didn't understand what he was saying. I had to make some excuse, go back upstairs, and look up "trollop" in my dictionary. Then I was twice as insulted, but the moment for a retort had passed.

Here's another incident I remember—in part because my mother has never let me forget it. One horrible, apocalyptic Saturday night when I was fifteen, I didn't have a date, and I was forced into the ignominy of going to the movies with my parents.

I agreed to do it, but only under certain conditions. I would drive downtown with my parents, but they had to let me off around the corner, two blocks from the theater, so I could arrive there without them. I would buy my ticket, go in, and save them two seats next to me . . . but they were to pretend they didn't notice me when they sat down. I also saved a seat on the other side of mine. That one would remain empty, so if anyone saw me, they would assume the seat belonged to my date, but he was just up getting me popcorn.

At the end of the movie, we were to leave the theater separately. My parents were to get the car and meet me around the corner. If any of my friends were around, they were to drive past and keep circling the block until the coast was clear.

My mother agreed to these terms, but only under one condition. She would remember this evening, and in years to come she would remind me of it.

Our system focuses on values: the value of money and how its real and symbolic value, as a medium of fair exchange, can be used as a basis for teaching your children values.

This book is about fair exchange as the basic medium for teaching your children social responsibility. It's not my place, or my desire, to tell you how you ought to think about issues of morality or religion, from dating practices to premarital sex and abortion. These are serious issues for other books and other discussions. I *do* believe that the techniques in this book are essentially communication techniques, and that if you can talk openly with your teenager about the subjects I have dealt with, it will help your communication in general.

There are financial repercussions to the abuse of drugs, to teenage drinking and driving, to teenage pregnancy, and to a wide variety of other forms of reckless or irresponsible behavior. But frankly, they are not the most important thing, and you shouldn't suggest to your teenager that you think they are, either before, during, or after a crisis. Your child's health and safety come first.

Nevertheless, your teenager should know that the consequences of his actions are potentially more far-reaching, even devastating, than they were when he was younger. A family attorney, doctor, or accountant can in many cases give sounder and more knowledgeable advice than you can. In fact, among the best things a parent can teach are research skills and where to go to find other resources for life skills information. I'll discuss all this in greater detail in my "Consequences of Actions" chapter. But teenagers, even as they move through a world governed by a bewildering set of rules that you can't begin to follow, are making their own ethical and logical decisions, and the more solid tools you give them, the more likely they are to use them.

Teenagers, in general, are interested in values. They're interested in fairness. And they're also interested in money. Their expenses are going up, and their ability to earn money is going up. So value, and the lessons of money as a medium for fair exchange, are going to be even more important as a communication tool.

Teenagers want to know more, they want to be trusted with more, and they want to be treated as your equal. In many ways, they deserve it. They *can* handle more responsibility and decision making, sometimes more than we give them credit for.

If you allow your teenagers—in fact, *encourage* your teenagers—to become fuller participants in the household, there's more chance that you can keep lines of communication open. There's less chance that they'll lose interest completely and slip away from you into a world that's governed entirely by peer pressure.

When does a child become a teenager? When does a teenager become an adult?

There are no hard and fast rules here; kids mature at different ages. Obviously there is no one creature that you can label a "teenager" and expect it to behave the same as every other teenager, or the same as itself for more than fifteen minutes at a time. Teenagers change drastically, suddenly, and constantly.

But in general we're counting the teenage years as those years with the word *teen* in them—thirteen through nineteen. In many religions, such as Judaism, the right of passage to adulthood, the Bar or Bat Mitzvah, comes at thirteen. Graduation from high school and the first year of college happens when a young person is eighteen or nineteen. So while these teenage exercises should be started whenever you and your child are ready for them, you should begin many of them, and start planning for when you'll begin others, when your child first enters those years that have "teen" on the end.

Welcome to the Planet Earth

Teenagers can still benefit from worksheets and exercises, but now their Citizen of the Household and Citizen of the Community responsibilities extend beyond games into real-life involvement.

In 1992 kids between the ages of twelve and nineteen spent $93 billion of their own and their parents' money. That is *real* life.

Teenagers live in a world that's part real life, part pure fantasyland: the world as they'd like it to be. There are bound to be some clashes between your view of reality and theirs, and the best way to deal with this is not to tell them in vague terms, "I know more about life than you do," but to *show* them how real life works, with numbers and specifics.

Teenagers think they'll earn a lot more money than they will.

The media is full of stories about incredible wealth, from Michael Jackson to Michael Milken to Michael Jordan— even a few people not named Michael, like Bill Gates. These are all relatively young people . . . role models, to use a vastly overused and abused term. Your teenager knows he's not likely to make as much money as Michael Jordan. But he doesn't necessarily know how great the difference will be.

Tad recalls playing the New York State lottery once. He had never played it before, and he won third prize. "It was a short, sweet, quickly disillusioned moment of excitement," he recalls. "I figured if first prize was ten million bucks, or however many million it was, third prize must be at least ten thousand dollars or so. When I went down to collect it, I discovered it was something like twenty-three dollars."

Your teenager may be harboring similar fantasies: maybe not Michael Jordan dollars, but a significant percentage of them.

When I was still president of The First Women's Bank, I began a program (which I've continued to this day) of working with inner-city teenagers, teaching them financial skills. One of the first questions they inevitably had was "How much money do you make?" So I turned it back on them: "How much do you think I make?"

I was shocked. All of their estimates were from a million to several million a year.

So I told them the truth, and they were shocked. "But that's not even enough to buy a Maserati!" I mean . . . I was president of a bank, then. A small bank, to be sure, but I was still making a respectable salary—unfortunately, only a tiny percentage of what they had expected.

Don't tell your teenager his Michael Jordan fantasies about how much he can make are full of (and inflated by) hot air. Let him find out for himself.

First, make a list of jobs or professions.

Next, have your teenager guess the average yearly income that can be made from this job or profession.

Next, have him research how much the real average yearly income is: for someone starting out in the field, for someone who has been in the field for ten years.

This is a valuable exercise in two ways. It will teach your teenager something about life on planet Earth, and it will teach him something about doing research, which will be an absolutely invaluable skill when he gets to college.

Make sure he does the entire exercise: it's not enough for him to find out the average yearly income for someone who has been in the field for ten years and then to assume he'll be making that straight out of college (or out of high school). Here are a few suggestions—add to them or change them, putting in the names of occupations engaged in by you, your family, and your friends.

Throughout this book we have alternated gender pronouns, because we firmly believe in complete gender equality, and we believe that values, and the life skills surrounding money, are completely gender neutral.

But for this exercise, have your teenagers research it both ways: How much money can a man expect to make for each of these occupations? How much money can a woman expect to make? Things are getting better these days, and many professions don't discriminate. But others still do.

Have your daughter do this exercise to get a realistic expectation of what she's up against.

Occupation	$ Per Year— Your Estimate	$ Per Year— Starting	$ Per Year — After Ten Years.
Auto Mechanic			
Garage owner			
Lawyer			
Accountant			
Store owner			
Teacher			
Computer programmer			
Coach			
Draftsman			
Architect			

Have your son do it, and make sure he knows that this is unfair and unacceptable; that we're working to build a world in which all prejudices, whether they are based on race, religion, sex, sexual preference, age, or physical handicaps, will be eliminated.

A recent *New York Times*/CBS News poll indicates that far too many teenage boys "still believe strongly in a traditional 1950s-style marriage, in which the wife stays home, rears the children, cleans the house, and does the cooking, while the husband is responsible for mowing the lawn."

Even though 71 percent of the teenagers had mothers who worked outside the home, only 58 percent of boys expected their future wives to work, as opposed to 86 percent of girls who expected to work. Perhaps this explains why, in the same survey, 38 percent of boys say they'd be missing an important part of life if they didn't get married, as opposed to only 26 percent of girls.*

It's important to show teenagers as well as telling them. Take them to your workplace. Let them see men and women working alongside each other, doing equal work, and let them see women in managerial positions.

New York Times, July 11, 1994, p. B11.

184 A Penny Saved

A lot of work still needs to be done in this area, but I have to note that we've won many battles already. In 1972, when I was a young executive with The Chase Manhattan Bank and the sole breadwinner in the family while my husband finished law school, not even Chase Manhattan would issue me a credit card in my name, only as Mrs. John Fraebel. That would never happen today.

Meanwhile we battle against the frustrations. The spelling check on Word for Windows refuses to recognize "superwoman" as a word. It flags it down as a misspelling and inquires if perhaps I don't mean "superman"?

I could add "superwoman" to the dictionary, but I choose not to. I leave it as a reminder of what still needs to be changed in the world.

Teenagers think they'll take home a lot more money than they will.
Take some of the occupations on the previous chart—the ones your teenager is most interested in—and put them into a second chart: this one for take-home pay. Again, the idea is for your teenager to guess first, then verify her guesses with research.

Occupation	Estimated Take-Home	Withholding Tax	FICA	Actual Take-Home

Teenagers think things cost a lot less than they do.
Most kids have little or no idea how much they would have to spend to live on their own. Have them estimate, then verify, how much these necessary living expenses cost per year.

Item	Estimated Cost	Real Cost
House		
Car		
Rent—studio apartment —city		
Rent—one-bedroom —small town		
Electricity		
Health insurance		
Car insurance		
Clothing		

None of this will entirely dispel a teenager's conviction that she knows more than you do, but we can't ask for miracles. It will give her a chance to find out, for herself, some solid information about the real world. And teenagers do learn. They're learning and absorbing all the time, even if they're not admitting it to you.

Citizen of the Household

As I was working on this chapter, a friend told me about a mutual acquaintance—I'll call her Sandra—whose teenage son, Pete, had switched the plates from her car to his unregistered car. His car then broke down by the side of the road, and he abandoned it. She told him to go back and get it towed, and he said sure, he'd get to it soon. By the time she gave up waiting for him and went out to find the car herself, it had been impounded by the police.

Sandra, a single mother who works hard running her own small business, is going to end up paying for it.

"Why doesn't she make Pete pay for it?" I asked.

"She doesn't 'make' him do things," my friend said wryly. "She's into treating him as an equal."

When I recovered from the enormity of this concept—that equals don't have to take financial responsibility for their own actions—I started thinking about what else Pete probably doesn't know and other ways he could learn from really being treated as an "equal."

Your teenager is old enough to understand how your household runs, how you budget for your family, and how your family's cash flow works.

Those exercises on how much people make, how much people take home, and how much people spend should make your teenager start to think about how adults live with money in the real world. I can't help wondering what kind of impact it would have on Pete if he were to sit down once a month with Sandra, if he were to write down the check stubs as she wrote out the checks, if he were to make the subtractions and write in the new balance brought forward after each check.

That's equality.

There's a special kind of financial reality in divorced households. Divorce makes children, and teenagers, feel powerless in the best of circumstances—as cut off from having a handle on their lives as their parents have cut themselves off from each other.

Teenagers are ready for the empowerment of knowledge here, too. There's nothing wrong with explaining the facts of child support, of who pays for what. It's part of your teenager's life; it affects her directly.

A major issue in household citizenship for teenagers is how much of a citizen does she still need to be? How much time should she still be expected to spend with the family? Of course, your teenager is still part of the household. Of course, she still has to abide by the family's rules. But her world is growing, as it should be, more and more outside the home. In a few more years she won't be part of the household. She'll be creating her own first household: with roommates in college, in an apartment of her own, with a significant other.

Your teenager should still be doing her Citizen of the Household chores. She should still be a part of family meetings. But she shouldn't be expected to do everything with the family. She's likely to be eating at home, then going to the movies with her friends. And if the family wants to go to Walt Disney World for the summer, and she wants to go on a teen tour of the West, you won't have to visit the Seven Dwarfs to see Grumpy if you insist on dragging her along.

Teens, of course, can't regulate their own behavior entirely. If you absolutely forbid your teenager to go to a music club with a reputation for serving drinks to minors, then he can't go.

Try not to have too many of those battles. As with your younger kids, you'll have rules that are negotiable and rules that are nonnegotiable. But don't expect it to be smooth sailing. Teenagers are guaranteed to insist on negotiating some of your nonnegotiable rules.

Rabbi Dworkin, who performed the wedding ceremony for two of my best friends recently, gave this rule of thumb for dealing with family problems, and it absolutely applies to dealing with teenagers: "Does it matter profoundly?"

In other words, you can still say no when your teenager asks if he can have a scorpion tattooed on his cheek.

But by the time he's in his teens, what's going to be tattooed on his soul—and that means loves and friendships, likes and dislikes, taste in music and clothes, cars and sports, and books and assorted extracurricular activities, whether he's a morning person or a night person—is his own.

Still, your teenager is living in your house and as such is a Citizen of the Household, with all the rules and privileges thereof.

I do believe, and strongly, that teenagers need to be disabused of the notion (which is a very easy one to fall into) that the family home has become Hotel Mom and Dad, with room service. As long as teenagers are living under your roof, Citizen of the Household rules should still apply.

Here are some of the house rules you should be able to set up and enforce for a teenager:

Curfew: These should be set according to the age of the teen and the standards of your household. Your teenager should take responsibility for keeping his own curfew.

Here's a good tip for making sure he does come in within the curfew and without your having to stay awake and check up. Put an alarm clock outside your bedroom door for each teenager. When he goes out, he has to set the clock to go off at the witching hour of his curfew. When he comes in (on time), he can turn off the alarm before it rings. If he doesn't come in on time, you'll know it.

Automobile: Of course, your teenager should obey *all* the rules of the road while driving the family car, from the speed limit to not picking up hitchhikers to no open containers. She should also be responsible for leaving the car the way she found it. This may include no half-empty potato chip bags on the floor, making sure the gas tank is refilled, and having the oil and windshield wiper fluid checked.

Parties: You don't have to let your teenager hold unchaperoned parties in your house. You don't have to let your teenager provide alcohol for underage party guests which is against the law! You can make a house rule against allowing other people to bring alcohol and/or drugs into a party at your house. You can also make a house rule that no kids who are already under the influence can be admitted into a party at your house. You have a very powerful argument on your side: providing alcohol to underage kids, or drugs to people of any age, is against the law.

Replacement: Teenagers have their own eating habits, and bless them for their cast-iron constitutions, but if your teen polishes off the last quart of milk in the refrigerator, you have a right to insist that he replace it. If your teenager borrows a ream of computer paper to print out her report that's due in the morning, she should replace that. You have a right never to be surprised that the last roll of toilet paper is gone and no one told you.

It's not okay: These are the major rules, the guidelines that you have to set according to your own conscience, your own religion, your own set of values. They include the big issues that parents have to wrestle with, from nicotine addiction to alcohol and illegal drugs, from early dating to teenage sexuality, from fighting to weapons. You know what's not okay, and you have a right, and a duty, to let your teenager know and to enforce those standards within the rules of your household. Grounding is a powerful tool in dealing with a teenager. The point is to make absolutely clear what "not okay" behavior is and to make provisions for responding to it within the boundaries of your house rules and the fair exchange of values.

Every household needs its own rules. Rules are subject to negotiation, especially as your children reach their teenage years (in family meetings or in ad hoc negotiation), but a household always runs on good citizenship, and good citizenship starts with a clearly defined, and evenly administered, code of conduct and justice.

Expanding Money Skills

By the time she's sixteen, your teenager should be off an allowance and working for herself. That $7-a-week allowance that seemed so generous for a seven-year-old has become a potential $16 a week, much less than a sixteen-year-old's earning capability through jobs she can find for herself.

Nor does she have to wait until she's sixteen. Tad's oldest daughter, now a lawyer, got her first job at age thirteen, when she went down to a restaurant in the small village where they lived and asked if they needed someone to launder their tablecloths and napkins for them.

In the economic sphere, your teenager is able to be a Citizen of the larger Community. In fact, you may be in competition for your teenager's work skills. She may be receiving better and more diverse openings for odd jobs, or part-time jobs, or entrepreneurial opportunities.

This doesn't mean that she's exempt from her Citizen of the Household responsibilities. It does mean that she's also a part of our free market economy, and it's perfectly just that the marketplace should decide where she peddles her services.

Fast-food franchises, stores, and restaurants are traditional employers of older teenagers, but before your child gets locked into a job of that sort, at minimum wage or not much more, sit down with her and explore other possibilities.

Here are some entrepreneurial options for your teenager. Use this as a springboard. Discuss it, either one to one or in a family meeting. You can come up with more, tailored to your teenager's particular skills or interests.

Lawn service
Pet sitting/walking/grooming
Snow removal
Baby-sitting

Birthday party planning
Coaching (baseball, tennis, rollerblading, other sports instru-
tion)
Computer tutor
Piano lessons
Art lessons
Chess lessons
Farm stand (grow and sell veggies)
Car wash
Read to kids
Garbage cleaning
Recycling service
Golf caddy
Academic tutoring
Pool cleaning
Video pickup and return
Specialized sales and import/export
Selling crafts on consignment

Here's what kids need to know about entrepreneurism in general.

It may not provide a regular income. Some entrepreneurs work for a long time "on spec" (on speculation). They are speculating that their work and their capital investment may work out.

For example, a skilled craftsperson—a weaver, let's say—may spend months preparing his work for a series of regional craft fairs during the summer. If those fairs are high-profile, high-volume events where only the best craftspeople are allowed to exhibit, he can—if he does well—make enough to sustain him for the rest of the year.

It depends on attracting customers. Your teen may think a car wash business is a great idea, but if not enough people know he's doing it—or if not enough people want to get their cars washed—he may not make enough money to justify his time. Successful entrepreneurism all depends on the entrepreneur.

It may be affected by local conditions. Your teen's car wash business can be adversely affected if four other teenagers in the same neighborhood get the same idea at the same time. It can be wiped out if there's a summer drought and the town declares a no-car-washing emergency.

Fortunately, not much overhead is invested in a business like this, and an enterprising teenage entrepreneur can recover quickly and try something else.

Remember, not everyone is cut out to be an entrepreneur. Some people like the security of a paycheck and can do their best, and rise to the top, in an organization. A teenager who goes to work at McDonald's and rises to assistant manager by the end of the summer may end up with more money in his pocket (and his savings account and his charity jar) than his entrepreneurial friend.

Don't bite off more than you can chew. A dog walking service is a good business for city or suburban kids, and there may be a demand for it in your neighborhood, but don't sign up a dozen dogs before you know for certain that you can handle four.

Here are a few tips on some other entrepreneurial ideas.

Recycling service. Many towns, cities, and villages have adopted new recycling regulations, and not everyone understands what they are or has the patience to follow them. That means there could be a lot of people willing to pay someone else to do it, and an enterprising teenager could make money and help the environment at the same time.

Birthday party planning. This is a real headache for lots of adults, but it could be a good business for a teen or a group of teens who have a flair for organization and relating to children and can demonstrate flair in festive-looking fliers and brochures.

Specialized sales and import/export. I knew a teenage boy who had a good knowledge of jewelry and had relatives in India. He combined these two assets to import jewelry and sell it to a number of local stores.

An upstate New Yorker told me that a lot of kids in his part of the country (near lakes and resorts) used to sell fishing worms. "But I went them one better. I started my own worm farm with special worms I imported from Georgia—Georgia jumpers, they were called. I found them in a catalog. I started when I was eight years old, and by the time I was sixteen I was able to buy myself a motorcycle. Actually, I got so successful so fast, it created a problem for me. My first year, after the word got around, one guy came up and wanted to buy a hundred worms from me, and I didn't know how to count up to a hundred."

Caddying. This is really more of a job than an entrepreneurial venture, but there's room for entrepreneurism within it. I heard of a number of very enterprising teenagers who found ways to parlay their caddying jobs into extra money. One group of young teenagers, after the golf course had closed for the evening, waded and dived into the pools and water hazards to bring up balls. They sorted out the ones that were still good, put them in egg cartons, and sold them at less than the retail price. After a while, golfers would put in orders for an egg carton full of their favorite brand. One of them recalls, "We were down in the pond by the twelfth fairway, and a club came sailing through the air and sank right in the middle of the pond. Then the golfer appeared. I guess he'd gotten pretty mad at that club, but now he was ready to forgive and forget. Only trouble was, the club was under six feet of water. We dove down and retrieved it for him, and he tipped us ten bucks."

An even better entrepreneurial scheme was dreamed up by a young man who went on to become the highly successful owner of his own business. He had invested in a stock of fifteen picnic coolers, and he bought ice and soda from a local beverage wholesaler. Every time there was a tournament or a major event at the country club where he caddied, he'd get the list of participants, contact them all in advance, and offer them his special service.

After he had interested a prospective client in his service, he'd find out how many were in his party. Then he'd fill a cooler with ice and soda and put it in a golf cart that he'd have cleaned and labeled with the name of the client, ready for him to drive off at tee time. He made enough money on this to start his first real business, an electronics repair business that needed capital for equipment, office space, and advertising. Not only the money he'd earned, but the connections he had made with older businesspeople on the golf course, proved invaluable to him in this new enterprise.

Snow removal. I talked to a former Bronxite about his teenage days, when he and his brothers figured out that stores needed their sidewalks clear all the time. "We'd shovel the snow as soon as it started piling up, for five dollars a storefront," he said. "Then if the snow lasted all day, we might shovel three, four, or five times at five dollars a pop for each store. I live in the country now—I don't know how country kids could ever make any money like we did."

Farm stand. A country girl who lives on the Maine coast I know laughed at that. "I don't know how city kids could make any money," she said. "Not the way I did. I had a little garden of snap beans, tomatoes, and corn. Those are the things people seem to buy most from a roadside stand. And my brother has a little dinghy, and he has five lobster traps. He gets leftover bait from the big lobster boats at the end of the day, and sets his little traps, and sells his five lobsters a day in the neighborhood."

Before They Leave the Nest

Living on your own is not just different from living at home, it's a *lot* different, even if you're prepared for it. If you're not prepared for it, it can be *shockingly* different.

My friend Beverly had a series of discussions with her sixteen-year-old daughter, Barbara, after Barbara had been grounded for an infraction that Beverly thought was quite serious. Barbara didn't agree.

"You can't ground me," Barbara said. "You don't understand. I *cannot* be grounded. I *have* to see my friends. My friends are the most important thing in the world to me, and nothing else comes second."

"If your friends are that valuable," Beverly said, "what are you willing to pay for them?"

"I don't buy my friends," Barbara said scornfully.

"No," said Beverly, "friendship isn't for sale, and it should never be. But there's still an exchange of values here. If being with your friends is so important to you, you have to pay the price of obeying our house rules so you won't be grounded."

"I can move out," Barbara informed her. "In six months I'll be seventeen, and then I can legally move out and get an apartment of my own."

Beverly didn't flat-out forbid her to do so—although that was certainly her first instinct. What she said instead was: "That's true. It is another price you can pay for the privilege of being with your friends. But let's see how high that price is. You do know you'll have to start paying your own car insurance."

"I will? Why?"

"You won't be living at this address anymore. We can't keep you on our policy. Besides, you want to be independent, don't you? Isn't that why you're moving out?"

Barbara was starting to turn pale by this time, but she stuck it out bravely. "Yes, it is. Well, I guess I can handle the car insurance."

"That's wonderful. I'm sure you can if you put your mind to it. By the way, what are you going to do about health insurance?"

"H-h-health insurance?"

"Sure. You know, as soon as the company I work for finds out you're not living at home with me anymore, they'll take you right off my health insurance policy."

Barbara's lip was quivering now. "Why do you have to *tell* everybody?"

Beverly had explained to her children that theft of services was stealing, just the same as shoplifting, but she explained it again to Barbara. Not telling the truth about someone moving out of your home would be theft of services, and it would be wrong.

"In this case," Beverly admits, "I was pleased that doing the right thing also coincided with doing what I really wanted to do, which was to throw roadblocks in the way of her moving out."

Barbara hasn't come right out and said yet that she's changed her mind about moving out. It's even possible (though unlikely) that she'll still go ahead and do it. If she does, Beverly knows that it won't be the end of the world. Barbara won't be a runaway; she'll still be living in the same town, and Beverly will know where she is. It's a rite of passage that all adolescents talk about and a few actually try out. And when Barbara finds out that the world is harder to live in than she had thought, she can still come back home—ideally with a greater understanding of what her mother goes through to run a household.

It *is* a painful and difficult experience for both parent and child if your new adult leaves home for real, to start college or get his first apartment, and he can't handle the business end of living on his own.

So here's a worksheet of life skills for your teenager to master while he's still living at home.

For each of the items on this worksheet, do the following:

Go over it with your teen for a dry run, as many dry runs as it takes him to get it right. Fill in the date of each practice session.

For some of the items, like balancing a checkbook, your dry runs can be the real thing; for others, like getting an account with the electric company, you can act it out.

When he's negotiated one of these life skills correctly with your help, check it off.

Next, have him do it on his own, without help. Here again, there'll be

LIFE SKILL	DONE WITH PARENT (DATE)	OK	DONE SOLO (DATE)	OK	DONE FOR REAL
Paying bills (1 month)					
Opening a checking account					
Opening a savings account					
Using an ATM machine					
Balancing a checkbook					
Stopping payment on a check					
Reordering checks					
Applying for a credit card					
Reading a lease					
Getting car insurance					
Getting a telephone installed					
Getting an account with the electric company					
Registering to vote (age eighteen)					
Getting a passport					
Following proper procedure in case of a car accident					
Applying for student aid (loans, scholarships, grants)					
Checking your credit report					
Buying insurance					
Building an investment portfolio					
Filling out an income tax form					

some variation, depending on the task. You can let him do the monthly bills by himself, though you'll want to double-check them before you send them off. On the other hand, it's conceivable that you might allow your teenager to have his own private phone line. In that case, he could check off not only "Done Solo," but also "Done for Real."

Some life skills will be "done for real" before your teenager leaves home; others will have to wait for his first real-life experience on his own. But he should be prepared for all of them.

Here are some more questions your teenager should be able to answer before she goes out on her own. Have her research and fill out the answers to each question.

Credit Cards

We're back full circle to the magic plastic card—and the scary thing is, many teenagers still seem to think that way. They do know that they'll have to pay for what they charge, but they don't know much more than that.

Here's what your teenager should know about credit cards:

The Five Commandments

1. Thou shalt keep all thy receipts when thou gettest thy bill. (This is so thou canst go over it and check off thy purchases to make sure that (a) thou didst not get charged for anything thou didst not buy, and (b) the figures for all thy purchases are correct.)
2. Thou shalt not charge if thou canst not pay in full at the end of the month.
3. Thou shalt not get into the habit of paying only the minimum balance at the end of the month.
4. Thou shalt not charge pizza (or any other perishables).
5. Thou shalt not charge thy card to the max (in case thou needest something for emergencies).

Many teenagers (and their parents, for that matter) may ask, "Why should I pay in full each month? Isn't it easier on the old bank account to just pay the minimum?"

The truth is, paying the minimum is one of the most expensive loans you'll ever take out.

1. The entries on my bank statement are (list and explain the meaning for each) :

2. Traveler's checks are:

2a. Here's how to get them:

3. Here's how they figure the minimum balance on my credit cards:

4. Here's what will happen if I don't pay the minimum balance on my credit cards:

5. These are the things I would need to know in order to decide if a prospective roommate is financially stable:

6. If I needed quick cash, I would:

7. If I lost my checkbook or credit cards, I would:

8. Tuition at my college of choice is $_____ per year.

9. Tuition at the local state college of choice is $_____ per year.

10. Other costs for a year at college are: _____
    Item _____ Cost _____
    _____ _____

11. My recource list for scholarships and student aid:

A typical $2,500 credit card bill, if you paid it off at the minimum each month, could take longer to pay off than a thirty-year mortgage.

Most credit card issuers require a minimum payment of only 2 percent to 2.5 percent of the new balance.

If you pay only the minimum each month—especially if you add even the tiniest new purchase—you'll be paying down the balance for decades.

Have your teenager figure out the true cost of a credit card purchase. In fact, this might be something she'd like to bring in and show her math teacher—it could be a class project.

This reminds me of a story that reinforces my point. Kids, if you give them the chance, will absorb more values than they let you know they're absorbing.

Eric was a teenager who came to one of my money skills workshops. His mother, Ruby, came with him to the first session. Ruby is a good woman and a conscientious mother who'd worked hard to instill values in Eric, but it was a frustrating task. Eric was street tough and cynical. He let me know by words and body language that he wasn't buying any of this jive.

I showed the class a video of one of my Oprah appearances—the one in which a teenager was disclaiming all responsibility for running up giant credit card bills. If they didn't want me to use the credit cards, her argument ran, they shouldn't have given them to me. It's not my fault— they're the ones who gave me the cards. "They" were her parents, the credit card companies—anyone but herself.

Eric spoke up. "I don't have a problem with that."

Ruby looked at me, and her eyes spoke volumes. *See?*

I was as concerned as she was. "You don't have any problem at all with it, Eric?"

"Nope. I don't have a problem with it. It's as simple as anything. If that girl ran up a credit card bill when she knew she didn't have the money to pay for it, it's stealing, just like if she went down to a store and took money out of the cash register."

I ran over and hugged him. Later I hugged Ruby. She had done her job as a mother, and it was starting to show.

Budgeting

Take special care with the budget your teenager creates and keeps for the last few years she spends in the shelter of your family. That's the budget format she'll take with her when she leaves home; and those first few years on her own are when she'll most need the stability and discipline of a solid budget.

Your teenager should be aware of the entire cost of her maintenance. That doesn't mean she'll have to pay for everything; you'll still be putting a roof over her head, paying the family grocery bill, and taking care of her health insurance and doctor bills. But she should be aware of these expenses: they are going to be hers soon enough.

There are two ways to make a budget. One is to figure out how much money you have and what you ought to be spending. If you were perfect, this would definitely be the best way, but few of us are perfect, and the problem with this method of budgeting is that we tend not to stick with it.

An alternative method is first to figure out your own spending profile, then tailor it, adapt it, rethink it to fit the amount of money you have to spend.

Start by having your teenager keep a spending notebook. This will be like the notebook she kept as a school-ager, described in the "Smart Consumer" chapter of the previous section, with one category added:

Day of the week: _____

Amount spent: $_____

Item bought: _____

Where bought: _____

Need or want: _____

Planned or impulse: _____

With . . . : _____

CATEGORY	DATE	ITEM	NEED/WANT	AMOUNT
Food				
			Total	
Clothing				
			Total	
Entertainment				
			Total	
Car				
			Total	
Sports and recreation				
			Total	
Accessories				
			Total	
Gifts				
			Total	
Phone				
			Total	
Other				
			Total	
			Total for Month	

"With . . ." means whom she was with when she bought it—for example: "boyfriend," "Amy," "a bunch of girls," "Mom."

Your teenager should keep her spending notebook for a month. Her expenses will be different from a school-ager's—they'll be larger, they'll cover more items, and a week won't be enough time to give her a realistic picture of her spending patterns.

Food Items

Item	N/W	$	Fast Food	Conv. Store	Rest.	Ent.

Other	Self	W/1	W/G	W/BF	Planned	Unpl. w/ Planned

Clothing Items

Item	N/W	$	Sale	Prem.	Sec. hand	In seas.
Other	Self	W/1	W/G	W/BF	Planned	Unpl. w/ Planned

A teenager's spending pattern is pretty much the same as everyone else's in one important respect. At the end of the month she's going to be saying, as we all tend to, "I don't understand it! Where did all the money go?"

With a monthly spending notebook, she'll start to know, and the two of you will be able to sit down and start analyzing it.

Here are some charted worksheets.

Entertainment Items

Item	N/W	$	Movie	Conc.	Arc.	Video	CD/Tape
Hardw.	Other	Self	W/1	W/G	W/BF	Planned	Unpl. w/ Planned

This will begin to give your teen an idea of where her money goes and how it's divided between wants and needs. Note that if a pattern starts developing under "other," she can create a new category. For instance, if she has an entrepreneurial occupation that she needs to buy supplies for, that would warrant a new category.

Car Items

Item	N/W	$	For Work	Destin.	Cruising	Other
Self	W/1	W/G	W/BF	Planned	Unpl.w/ Planned	

Sports and Recreation Items

Item	N/W	$	Usage	Equip.	Other
Self	W/1	W/G	W/BF	Planned	Unpl.w/ Planned

There are more ways she can analyze her spending patterns.

For each item, enter the amount of the purchase and whether it was a need or a want. Then check the kind of establishment it was bought in: a fast-food store, a convenience store, a restaurant, an entertainment venue (a movie, a concert, a ball game, miniature golf), or another location.

Was she alone when she made the purchase? With one friend? With a group of friends? With her boyfriend? Tell her to make a note, as well, if she picked up the tab for some or all of her friends. If so, is this arrangement a reciprocal one? Do they pick up the tab for her on other occasions? If she's not sure, this is another thing to track.

Was the purchase planned or unplanned? If it was unplanned, was it made as part of a shopping trip where she had gone out to make a planned purchase?

Accessories

Item	N/W	$	Pers. Hygiene	Batteries Etc.	Jewelry	Grooming
Clothing	Self	W/1	W/G	W/BF	Planned	Unpl. w/ Planned

Here, "Sale" means the item was on sale. "Prem." means it was a premium item and she paid more for it because it was a designer label or brand name. "Secondhand" means a secondhand, yard sale, or thrift shop item. "In Seas." means the article was bought in season: for example, a bathing suit in the summer.

Here the categories are movies, concerts, arcades, video rentals, CDs and tapes, and hardware—a Walkman, a CD player, VCRs, and so on. These categories can be tailored by your teenager to fit her own interests.

She can divide her car usage into driving for work (or school), driving with a particular destination in mind, or just driving around.

Usage includes everything from tennis court fees to miniature golf to entry fees for a seventy-mile whitewater canoe race. Equipment is the hardware of sports: golf clubs, specialized athletic shoes, rock climbing ropes, and pitons.

The individual categories here represent whom the gifts are for.

If your teenager calls certain people often over long distance, she should know who they are and how much money she spends on them.

With this much data, your teenager should be able to make a very detailed analysis of her spending profile.

A final worksheet will put this into perspective for her.

Item	N/W	$	For:			

Self	W/1	W/G	W/BF	Planned	Unpl.w/ Planned	

After she's made out this chart, she'll be able to answer the question, "Where does the money go?" and she'll also be able to figure out how it happens to go there.

Phone Items

Item	N/W	$	Basic	Calls to A (min.)	Calls to B (min.)	Calls to C (min.)	Others

Maxie's Spending Profile

1. I spend most on:
    1. _____
    2. _____
    3. _____

2. Most of my unplanned
   purchases are:
    1. _____
    2. _____
    3. _____

3. I make most of my unplanned
   purchases when:
    1. _____
    2. _____
    3. _____

4. I get most satisfaction from:
    1. _____
    2. _____
    3. _____

She can compare her answers to question 1. and question 4. If they're different—if where she gets the most satisfaction and where she spends the most money are not the same—then she has a really good idea of where to start cutting down if she has to tighten her budget.

Making the Budget

Now she's ready to make a budget.

A budget is a pretty simple matter. All you do is total up the money you have coming in, subtract your need spending (your fixed expenses), and fit your want spending into whatever money you have left.

What makes it harder for a teenager is that she'll be taking on new expenses, expenses that you formerly paid.

This is part of the gradual phasing out of your teenager's dependence on you and her moving toward the complete independence of adulthood.

Phasing Out

Your teenager should understand the entire cost-of-living picture, even though he won't be shouldering all those expenses right away.

So when you sit down to help him make up a budget, it should be a budget that he'll be able to take with him when he leaves home and a budget that reflects the entire financial burden of his existence.

This doesn't mean you're suddenly going to start charging your four-teen-year-old rent or expecting your sixteen-year-old to pay his own doctor's bills. It does mean that he should know what those bills are and what part of his financial picture they make up.

Gradually, all the bills that represent expenditures on your teen-ager will become the responsibility of your teenager, in two different ways.

First, he will become more and more responsible for paying his own expenses.

Second, he will become more and more responsible for managing the money that pays his expenses. For many of the expenses you still assume, you'll put the money in his account, and he'll write the checks.

Here is a series of sample budgets for your teenager. Why a series? Simple: As your teenager grows up, he'll have more money; he'll have different expenses; most important, he'll be taking on more responsibility. So, the budgets will change accordingly. That's why we call them the "phase budgets"—they track the phasing out of parental responsibility, the phasing in of new adult responsibility.

These figures are composites, based on the family budgets of selected teenagers; they'll be different for each family, and the breakdown between parent and child will be whatever a family chooses to make it.

The point here is, if you make up all of these phase budgets in advance, both you and your teenager will have a blueprint for his increasing responsibility for his own fiscal life.

Beyond the Jar System

Your post-sixteen-year-old teenager is off allowance and making his own money. He's outgrown the jar system of apportioning, too—up to a point.

He no longer has to be told to divide his money between quick cash and medium-term savings. Those are his decisions now.

Once he starts filing a real federal income tax form of his own, he is no longer responsible for paying family tax, although he'll still have to contribute if he wants to be part of a family vacation.

He still has to put money into his long-term savings for college.

Charity becomes his own choice now. You can let him know that you hope he'll continue to put aside 10 percent of his income for charity, either the family charity or one of his own choosing.

Maybe you won't even have to tell him. As I've said before, charity doesn't start out as a natural instinct, but it can become a deeply ingrained part of your spirit.

My friend Spencer Christian, weatherman and TV personality for *Good Morning America*, came from a background of extreme poverty, and he has never forgotten how important it is to give back to those less fortunate. He told me that what's most rewarding to him is that his children, who grew up with plenty, have the same commitment. Spencer's son, Jason, was offered an academic scholarship to college but turned it down. Spencer, the proud father, couldn't believe it. Jason had earned it. He had finished at the top of his class, he had won the scholarship competitively, on merit.

"That's true, Dad, but I don't need it," Jason said. "The honor is satisfaction enough for me. I'd rather it go to someone who can't afford college without it."

Spencer was even prouder.

Real-World Situations

Your teenagers are going to be adults with homes of their own someday, and those homes are going to need all the things that your home needs: plumbers and plasterers, electricians and TV repairmen.

Jason's Annual Phase Budget—Age Fourteen

Income	$	Expense Item	$	Parents' %	Jason's %	Who Writes the Check	Contributing to Checking Account	
							Parent	Jason
Odd jobs	450	Clothing	1,200	90	10	Jason	1,080	120
After-school job		School supplies	150	100	0	Jason	150	0
Summer job	522	Gifts	300	20	80	Jason	60	240
Gifts from relatives	300	Entertainment	500	20	80	Jason	100	400
Allowance (work for pay)	728	Car insurance	N/A					
		Gas	N/A					
		Car upkeep	N/A					
		School lunch	400	100	0	Jason	400	0
		Charity	200	0	100	Jason	0	200
		Rent	2,400[1]	100	0	Parent	2,400	0
		Utilities	300[2]	100	0	Parent	300	0
		Phone bill	150[3]	80	20	Parent	120	30
		Groceries	1,500	100	0	Parent	1,500	0
		Savings	720[4]	0	100	Jason	0	720
		Family tax	290	0	100	Jason	0	290
Total	2,000	Total	8,110				6,110	2,000

1. Based on a percentage of the family's total cost for these items.
2. Based on a percentage of the family's total cost for these items.
3. Based on $120 a year as a percentage of the family's basic bill, $30 a year as teenager's long-distance calling.
4. Based on $480 long-term savings plus $480 medium-term savings (percentage of income) minus $240 gifts, which would come out of medium-term savings.

Jason's Phase Budget—Age Sixteen

Income	$	Expense Item	$	Parents' %	Jason's %	Who Writes the Check	Contributing to Checking Account Parent	Contributing to Checking Account Jason
Odd jobs	700	Clothing	1,500	80	20	Jason	1,200	300
After-school job	1,100	School supplies	200	100	0	Jason	200	0
Summer job	2,000	Gifts	500	0	100	Jason	0	500
Gifts from relatives	400	Entertainment	1,000	0	100	Jason	0	1,000
		Car insurance	700	50	50	Parent	350	350
		Gas	500	0	100	Jason	0	500
		Car upkeep[5]	400	80	20	Jason	320	80
		School lunch	400	100	0	Jason	400	0
		Charity	450	0	100	Jason	0	300
		Rent	2,400	100	0	Parent	2,400	0
		Utilities	300	100	0	Parent	300	0
		Phone bill	200	60	40	Jason	120	80
		Groceries	1,500	100	0	Parent	1,500	0
		Savings	1,000[6]		100	Parent	0	0
Total	4,200		11,050				6,790	3,110

5. Includes regular maintenance such as oil change, tune-up, new tires, car wash. One of your teenager's Citizen of the Household chores, as a new driver, will be to take the family car in for all of these.

6. Long-term saving only.

Jason's Phase Budget—Age Nineteen (At College)

Income	$	Expense Item	$	Parents' %	Jason's %	Who Writes the Check	Contributing to Checking Account	
							Parent	Jason
Odd jobs	0	Clothing	1,500	40	60	Jason	600	900
After-school job	3,500	School supplies	700	50	50	Jason	350	350
Summer job	3,750	Gifts	500	0	100	Jason	0	500
Gifts from relatives	1,250	Entertainment	1,500	0	100	Jason	0	1,500
Parent subsidy	2,700	Car insurance	700	0	100	Parent	0	700
		Gas	800	0	100	Jason	0	800
		Car upkeep[5]	2,400[7]	0	100	Jason	0	2,400
		School lunch						
		Charity	650	0	100	Jason	0	650
		Rent	4,400[8]	100	0	Jason	4,400	0
		Utilities						
		Phone bill	400	0	100	Jason		400
		Groceries	1,000	50	50	Parent	500	500
		Savings	2,500					
Total	11,200		17,050				5,850	8,700

7. Includes buying own car.
8. Includes fees for college room (plus meal money and utilities)

Give your teen some exercise in dealing with these real-world situations.

Pipes are going to burst. When they do, have her join you as you go through the routine of dealing with it.

First, make sure she knows the house. Where are the circuit breakers? Where is the shut-off valve for the water? Is there more than one shut-off valve, so you don't have to cut off the water for the whole house if something is leaking out of control in the kids' bathroom? Where's the reset button for the hot-water heater?

If she's home when the pipe bursts, you can send her to shut off the water.

Then have her with you, or on an extension, when you call the plumber. Make her part of the endeavor when the plumber comes, outlines the job to you, and gives you an estimate. After he leaves, discuss with your teenager how the transaction went, and decide whether you need to get a second estimate.

Bring your teenager with you when you go to shop for a car, or a second mortgage, or a builder to redo the basement.

Discuss ahead of time what you're going to do.

The important thing to remember in going out to make a major purchase is to stay focused. Remember what your goal is, and keep your attention on it at all times. Don't get distracted by "form vs. substance" issues. For example, when you're buying a car, don't try to impress the dealer with knowledge you don't have—you're playing in his ball park then.

Do know exactly what you want before you go in: what models you've narrowed your choice to, what price range, what options. Remember what your goals are. They may be (a) to leave with a new car, and (b) to get the lowest price. Or if you're still shopping around, they may be (a) to leave without making any commitment at all, and (b) to find out how good a deal the dealership will give you.

Incidentally, you don't have to be Superwoman (or even Superman, whoever he is) to teach lessons to your kids. It's okay if you're not perfect at all these things. In fact, you can even make a game of it.

This one works particularly well if you have a couple of teenagers (good luck to you). Bring them along when you go to the car dealership, or the architect, or the computer store. Have them take notes. Afterward let them judge you, holding up scorecard numbers like figure-skating judges, on such criteria as:

1. Did the contestant ask questions based on her needs?
2. Did the contestant succeed in getting satisfactory responses about size, gasoline mileage, safety factors, warranty, price range, and so on?

It's fun. It gives the kids a sense of empowerment without stripping you of any serious dignity. And it might teach all of you something.

Investments

Not everyone is going to want to invest, but everyone should know how it works. It's one more thing that money can do, another panel in the whole picture of money as a life skill.

It's an empowering skill. It's a real adult activity, one that teenagers often take an interest in. It feels like something that grown-ups do.

As adult activities go, it's safer and more productive than smoking cigars out behind the barn. But it does take some knowledge and some prudence.

Here's a little quiz on the stock market for your teenager to take. I've included the answers, of course, but let her try her hand at the questions first.

Answers

1. **Investing** is when you lend money to someone else who uses your money and pays you for the use of it.
2. A **stock,** itself, is a piece of paper, called a **stock certificate.** It's what it stands for that counts. It represents ownership in a company. For the company, the purpose of selling **shares of stock,** or part ownership in their business, is to raise money to use in the business.

   The reason people (or companies) buy stock is that they're making an **investment.** They (or their stockbrokers) have studied the company, and they believe that the company will use the money in a smart way, so that the value of the company will go up and the price of the shares will rise, too.
3. A **stockholder** is anyone who owns shares of stock. A stockholder is a part owner of the company and can vote her shares on

Stock Market Quiz

1. What is investing? _____

_____

_____

2. What is stock? _____

_____

_____

3. What is a stockbroker? What do they do? _____

_____

_____

4.How do you make money as a stockbroker? _____

_____

_____

OTHER TYPES OF INVESTMENTS

5. What is a bank savings account? _____

_____

_____

6. What is a bond? _____

_____

_____

7. What is a mutual fund? _____

_____

_____

certain company issues, such as who will sit on the **board of directors** of the company. "Voting one's shares" means that the stockholder gets one vote for each share she holds. If she holds ten shares of Reebok, for instance, she controls ten votes (in the case of Reebok, that would be ten out of a total of about 113 million).

4. Let's say a teenager does buy ten shares of Reebok. He wears them, his friends wear them. He likes the product, and his financial adviser tells him the company is well managed. If it turns out that the two of them are right, and a lot of teenagers think they'd look great and run fast in Reeboks, the company will make a profit. Some companies share that profit with their stockholders in the form of **dividends.** These are called **income stocks.**

Other stocks are called **growth stocks.** Growth stock companies put the profits back into the company instead of paying dividends. This makes the value of the company greater. Then more people will decide the company is a good investment, and they'll want to buy stock, too. Then the **demand** for the stock will be greater, and the price of a share will go up. If the teenager decides to sell his stock, he'll make a profit.

On the other hand, if Reebok starts losing sales, and they take a loss, a lot of people will want to sell the stock, and not so many will want to buy it. The price will go down.

5. With a **bank savings account,** you deposit your money in a bank, and the bank uses it to make loans to other people for things like cars and home mortgages. When you deposit your money in a bank, you are in effect lending it to the bank, and the bank pays you interest on it.

6. A **bond** is a certain type of loan, taken out by a large company or a government, which guarantees to pay back the loan (bond) over a period of time, with interest.

7. A **mutual fund** is a group of stocks, bonds, and other securities run by professional **money managers,** whose job is to help you take the guesswork out of investing. Mutual funds are designed to be safer investments, because they can buy a greater number of diversified securities than most individual investors could afford to own.

Starting a Portfolio

If your teenager is interested, let him start his own portfolio, or collection of stocks.

A good way to start is by tracking a few companies that are associated with products he knows—Reebok, McDonald's, Disney, to name a few.

Another good way—popular with idealistic teenagers—is to do a little research and create an *environmentally conscious portfolio*—companies like Ben & Jerry, Esprit, and Levi-Strauss, known to have a good record on environmental issues.

Then have your teenager look up the companies on the stock pages of the newspaper and show him how to read the symbols on the page. Explain to him that the daily stock quotation is only a record of how the stock did that day. Just because Disney happens to go up three points on the first day he looks at it doesn't mean it's going to continue doing that.

He'll have to investigate further. At the local public library, he should find the *Value Line Investment Survey*, which will give him analysts' reports on every company traded on the stock exchange. He can also get information from *S&P Reports* and *Moody's Handbook of Common Stocks.*

If you have a stockbroker, take your teenager to visit her and have her explain to him how she evaluates stock and what she thinks of the ones he has chosen. If for some reason she thinks they're a poor investment, she can explain why and perhaps recommend other, similar stocks.

Then have your teenager place her order—through you. You'll have to put the account jointly in your name and hers until she's twenty-one.

If you don't have a broker, you can use a discount brokerage house.

Have your teenager track the stock once a week. Have him read the company's annual report.

Here's a form he can use:

Tracking Sheet for _____/_____
                        (name of corporation/ abbreviation)
                              Date   Price

Bought: _____   _____

Price Checked: _____   _____

                           _____   _____

                           _____   _____

                           _____   _____

Have your teenager research and report back to you on other investment vehicles, such as mutual funds and bonds.

A stock can also make a good holiday gift. Tad recalls that one year, when his daughter Wendy was a teenager, he gave her a gift (approved by his financial planner) of stock in Wendy's restaurants.

Make sure your teenager knows how to include all stock dividends and transactions on her income tax return.

Facing the World

Dress for Success

I've pointed out that many rules change with the teenage years. Your child is now making most of his own spending decisions and a lot of his other decisions, too.

That doesn't mean he's not a Citizen of the Household, because he still is. He's still expected to be a contributing member of the family and fulfill his obligations to Citizen of the Household chores.

He's still subject to some rules that are negotiable and some rules that are nonnegotiable.

The trouble is, your teenager is going to have much more of a mind of his own in this arena. He's going to start negotiating some of those nonnegotiable issues. And sometimes you're going to have to bend.

Rabbi Dworkin's rule here is the best one to follow: "Does it matter profoundly?"

Clothing is going to be one of these issues.

Clothing is an important part of a teenager's self-expression, and often it's hard to give up. In the sixties we thought we'd never have to put away our tie-dyes and bell-bottoms to join the Establishment. In the nineties kids feel the same way about their baseball caps turned backward and their baggy shorts that come down to their ankles.

It doesn't matter profoundly if he goes to his first job interview dressed inappropriately. This is (on a larger scale) like selling Mighty Max for three dollars in the schoolyard. It's unfortunate, but he can live with (and learn from) the consequences.

It does matter profoundly if he insists on expressing himself at an important family function—a wedding, or a funeral, or a grandmother's birthday. Most teenagers will understand this. Even if they're rebelling a whole lot against your rules, they generally remain pretty faithful to "Grandma rules." If there is a problem, you must remind them that these are Citizen of the Household duties, and they're important ones. People's feelings are at stake.

Your teen may understand that Grandpa's and Grandma's feelings are important, but he may not always understand what they are. You can try to explain to him that the issue of clothes sometimes bears a direct correlation to age. As you get older, the way people dress starts to seem like more of a symbol of how the family is doing.

Some grandparents seem to think that if their grandchildren are well dressed, clean, and with tidy hair, it's a sign that the family is stable. A sloppy grandchild sends an alarm signal: "trouble at home, divorce, money problems . . ."

Remind your kids that their grandparents didn't have the same kinds of choices they have now. In their grandparents' era, a kid with a nose ring and pink hair couldn't have made it into a good college.

You should not, however, make your teenager financially responsible for a wardrobe he doesn't like. The dark suit for weddings and funerals should be your expense. It's only fair.

Ultimately your child will learn for herself that she has to dress for success. There's a hilarious *Saturday Night Live* routine about a group of college girls sitting around the sorority house in their baggy shorts and sweatshirts, talking unintelligible slang in Valley Girl accents. A sorority sister who's graduated the year before comes back to visit. She's dressed in a suit and heels, with a conservative hairdo—and at first they're suspicious of her. But she starts prattling away in Valley Girl talk, and they welcome her with open arms.

Then her beeper goes off. She calls the office, and instantly she's a professional woman—concise, articulate, dynamic, intelligent. When she gets off the phone, she tries talking Valley Girl–ese again, but it's no use. They know she's a traitor.

The point is, all teenagers think they'll never grow up, and they all know, deep down inside, that they will grow up. And they all *do* grow up.

It's always been that way, even in the sixties. Tad remembers passing a young man in a homburg, dark suit, and briefcase on a New York street. The man hailed him, and Tad did a double take when he realized he had seen him, two weeks earlier, with a scraggly beard and bell-bottoms in a hippie crash pad in upstate New Paltz.

I even did it myself. For a few months after I went to work for Chase Manhattan, I would put on jeans, take off my makeup, and spend week-ends with my old college pals—not telling them what I was doing during the week. I finally got caught when someone noticed my nails were manicured.

I volunteer my time regularly teaching entrepreneurial skills to a group of teenagers in New York City's Harlem. These are bright, ambitious, and talented kids, but many of them tend to feel that their hip-hop clothing represents a culture of which they're understandably and justifiably proud. They resent being told that they have to dress up in stiff, unfamiliar, and "Establishment" clothing.

I've pointed out to them—and it's worked pretty well—that Patrick Ewing puts on white shorts and an undershirt with blue-and-orange trim when he goes to work, but those aren't the clothes he wears on the street. Deion Sanders puts on pants with elastic on the bottom and a shirt with an insignia on the front for one of his jobs and padded pants, shoulder pads, and a helmet for the other. He doesn't wear either of those outfits on the street. Wearing what's expected of them is part of their commitment to the work environment, even if they happen to be multimillionaire athletes.

Many of the rest of us wear uniforms at some point in our lives, whether we're soldiers, police officers, or McDonald's employees. It doesn't mean we lose ourselves in our clothes. Maybe we are what we eat, but we don't have to be what we wear.

Thinking about Success

Kids tend to see themselves, in some vague future, as extremely successful. This fantasy, or visualization, may be about a career that they are ultimately going to follow, or it may be about a pipe dream. The career ambition may change every week, but the dreams are always grand, as dreams should be.

If this week your teenager wants to be an actress, she no doubt sees herself as accepting the Academy Award. If she wants to be a doctor, she sees herself accepting tearful thanks and hearty congratulations for a brilliant and difficult heart transplant. If she wants to be a politician, she sees herself being sworn in as president of the United States. (Incidentally, this isn't restricted to teenagers. I was invited to Washington recently to meet with President and Mrs. Clinton to discuss the health care plan, and as I walked up the front walk to the White House, I realized I was mentally redesigning it for when I was President—the stables will go over there, the riding ring will be over here . . .)

What do all these fantasies have in common?

They're all about *being*.

And a real career—a real, rewarding career—is all about *doing*.

This is an important lesson for your teenager to absorb. The career she'll want to devote her life to (or a portion of her life; changing careers in midlife has become a part of the American experience) is the career that offers an absorbing journey, not a glittering destination.

Give your teenager a research assignment. Have him interview four or five people he admires, and ask them two questions:

1. What does success mean to you?
2. What do you find rewarding/unrewarding about your career?

Then tell him to assume that he has no preconceptions: that he came into this research project with no ideas of his own on the subject. Have him build a theory, based entirely on the answers he gets, about the meaning of success and achievement in life.

Talk to him about the results of his research. Make sure he understands that success is personal and measured by one's own feeling of achievement, not by material reward alone.

Conflict Management

As I've stated before, your teenager is going to start negotiating the nonnegotiable.

As she gets older, very little is really nonnegotiable. There are important Citizen of the Household issues that she'll have to abide by as long as she's living under your roof, and these can be negotiated up to a point, but ultimately you make the house rules. Still, she's going to be an adult soon, and then *every* decision will be her own.

So it's wise to listen and respond thoughtfully to every conflict.

Let's take a big one: "I've decided I'm not going to college."

What could be more nonnegotiable than that? Ever since she's been three years old (or whenever you started on the jar system) she's been putting away a percentage of her money in her long-term savings for college. That was always nonnegotiable.

So what do you do?

You listen and discuss it with her calmly. Keep in the back of your mind (a) that this is only one of a number of scenarios that she's considering, and (b) that you can influence her, but if her mind is absolutely made up not to go to college, you can't force her to go.

Remember that a picture is worth a thousand words, and a picture your kid draws for herself is worth ten thousand. Have her research or research together—the jobs you can get, the careers you can have, with or without college. Don't try to propagandize too heavily. Don't pretend that there aren't CEOs of major companies who never went to college—she'll find them by herself, anyway. You might point out that most of them are older and that this kind of career without a degree is a much harder route to take these days. Then again, perhaps you're better off letting her figure out even that part for herself.

At this point, faith becomes the magic word. If you've raised your child with a good set of values, those values have been internalized. They're in there somewhere, and even if they're rattled around for a while by the winds of rebellion, they're not going to be blown away for good. Even if she says, "I'm going to be one of the tiny fraction who becomes a millionaire/ballerina/explorer/artist without going to college," she'll still be noticing—and filing away—that it is only a tiny fraction.

Remember, you've also raised your child to think for himself.

Okay, let's take a few scenarios.

"I've decided I'm not going to go to college, I'm going to be a rock star."

Who's saying this? This is probably a young teenager, a thirteen- or fourteen-year-old. It's a dreamy, young-teenage statement. An eighteen-year-old isn't going to suddenly decide to be a star—either he's been playing music for awhile and has decided (or been told that) he has the talent and the interest to pursue it, or he hasn't.

Your thirteen-year-old also doesn't have a clear sense of college, or of not going to college, for that matter, so this is all likely to change. You can't tell him that. But you can tell him something about the economics of business, and you can talk to him about the range of skills he'll need to succeed in the business.

We talked to Don Bell, now a financial planner but through the 1970s and early 1980s a serious musician who reached a significant level of regional success, about the business end of a career in rock and roll.

"For the early stages—his high school career—the opportunities to play will be limited, and the venues he'll play in—school dances, mostly—won't expect much of him, so his outlay for equipment will be minimal—he'll need an instrument, an inexpensive amplifier, and a minimal sort of PA system. Kids tend to think they need more, but they don't. Most of the places he'll be playing, like the high school gym, will have some sort of PA system in place.

"He'll need to get a group of kids together to form a band, and the principal managerial skill he'll need here is patience and the ability to tolerate a lot of frustration. These are, incidentally, qualities he'll continue to need. I'm assuming that he's the one kid in a hundred who'll stick with it, which means that most of his friends won't. So he's going to have to deal with the fact that most of his friends, when they find out how hard it is and how much practice it takes, will drop out fairly quickly. (Here's a helpful hint: If your kid wants to be a musician, encourage him to be a guitar player. A beginning band will always practice at the drummer's house.)

"I grew up in Saugerties, New York, in the early seventies, and Saugerties is right next to Woodstock, so you know there was a high level of musical consciousness. And in a school of about eighteen hundred kids, there were two bands; that means a maximum of ten or eleven kids playing seriously.

"Okay, he's a little older now, and he really wants to make a commitment to playing seriously.

"First, he has to decide what kind of music he's going to play. If he wants to play a sort of easy listening style of music, the investment is still relatively small. Again, he'll be playing in a lot of venues that will be set up already, so he'll only need his own equipment and a small PA.

"But you said this kid wants to be a rock star. So to play in a rock band—to build a reputation, to make it viable—that takes a serious capital outlay. He'll need better equipment and an expensive PA system, maybe five to ten thousand dollars. Of course, this is a band expense—he won't have to shoulder it alone. And he'll need a van to carry the equipment to gigs.

"Those are the major expenses. But there are more. His band won't be able to practice in the drummer's garage all the time—it won't be enough. He'll have to book time at a rehearsal studio. He'll have to make demo tapes—he can do that at the rehearsal studio, so again it's not a major expense, especially if he learns something about studio work and maybe even a little engineering.

"He'll have to pay to get copies made of the tape. He'll have to find out who books live music in the area, but this is not really expense—just the cost of a newspaper.

"Let's assume he's the group's business manager, too—because he can't assume that someone else will be. So he'll have to start booking the band. That means calling all the local clubs, talking to the club managers, making appointments to come down and see them and leave them your tape.

"Then, if they like you, they'll say, 'Yeah, come in Wednesday night. You can work for the door.' That means you don't get paid, but you do get whatever cover charge the club charges at the door. If it's two bucks a head, and a hundred people come in, your band will be dividing two hundred dollars.

"So now he's a professional musician. If he keeps at it, keeps getting his tapes around, plays more clubs, starts getting a local following, has a reasonable amount of success, he can expect to earn back his capital outlay in a year, maybe a little less.

"Then he can make a successful living for a while—maybe a thousand dollars a week net, or close to it. That's after expenses and before taxes.

"Now the business end of it involves keeping a ledger sheet. Dividing up the money is relatively easy—you do it each night after the gig, in cash, and after expenses are deducted. So someone has to keep an itemized list of expenses, with receipts. Your personal expenses are separate—guitar strings, a new fuzztone pedal. Band expenses include everything from gas to light bulbs to dry ice for fog effects—that was a *very* big expense, back in the seventies.

"Who owns the van the band uses? If the band owns it, how is it registered and insured? If you own it, what percent of its use goes to band business, what percent to your personal business? Is there an agreement with the band about a certain percentage of auto repairs and maintenance coming out of band overhead?

"For income tax purposes, you have to keep records of your income and expenses, which can include clothing, travel, a per diem on the road.

"You can go to college and work full-time in a band—I did it—but it's hard. Well, lots of ways of making a living are hard."

Don has two young children, a boy and a girl. Would he let them go into that life?

"If they had the talent and the determination, I'd say sure, go for it. The world needs more musicians and poets and artists. It's in danger of losing its soul."

"I've decided I really want to pursue a career in music."

This is a different story. This is your eighteen-year-old, your high school graduate, who's already found out for herself (or with your help) all the things that you had to tell the thirteen-year-old dreamer. She's been playing with a band, she's had some success, she's ready to make the next move.

Again, if her mind is made up, you may not be able to stop her (like Don Bell, you may not even want to). But decisions still must be made. Does pursuing a career in rock and roll mean postponing college? Or will she use it as a way to help pay for college?

You can't negotiate her heart or her burning ambition. You can still negotiate your financial involvement with her. Suppose, because of her rock and roll career, it takes her six years to finish college? Will you pay what you would have paid for four years and leave it up to her to make up the difference? Does she need a loan to pay for equipment? On what terms will she pay it back?

These are negotiations between the two of you, and there are no right or wrong answers. What's important is to negotiate in good faith and make sure all negotiable items—that is to say, all items involving the exchange of value, either money or time—are covered.

"I want to take a year off and go to Europe before I start college."

You have a right to know why he wants to do this. It might be an important part of his education—not all education comes from college classrooms. In fact, every college professor I've ever talked to has praised the work ethic and worldview of returning students.

Based on your discussion of his plans, you can decide to what extent you want to get financially involved with this project. Does he plan to finance it himself? In that case you might agree on leaving his college money in an interest-bearing vehicle for another year. If you think this European trip is truly educational, you might even agree to go on adding to it at the same rate you have in the past—you'd probably also expect him to keep contributing a percentage of anything he earns to his college savings.

Again, time and money are value items, and they can be negotiated as value transactions, not as a referendum on who's a good person.

Once again, I emphasize faith and trust. Trust is built incrementally, over a period of time. And just as it's built incrementally, if it has to be withdrawn, that should be incremental as well. "You want to go bumming around Europe? Well, forget it—I'm withdrawing your college fund!" is not appropriate.

Remember the family bank loans? You didn't cancel your child's allowance forever for defaulting on a loan; you had an appropriate, built-in penalty. That's even more important in negotiating with older kids, when independence issues are so strong and feelings can run high.

Consequences of Actions

All actions have their natural consequences. I've talked about this throughout the book: Children need to learn that the natural consequence of saving is making money (interest added), and the natural consequence of borrowing is losing money (interest paid out). They need to learn that the natural consequence of carelessness is an accident, and the natural consequence of accidental breakage is monetary.

As children get older, natural consequences become more far-reaching. Parents worry about children at every age, of course, and with good reason. Children at any age can get hurt, and even young children can set off an incredible chain of events. But teenagers have many more opportunities to get in a *lot* of trouble. (Remember my "tractor in the pond" story?)

Teenagers are going to be eligible (exact age varies from state to state) to get a driver's license, and this opens up not only large areas of freedom, but large areas of responsibility—for both you and your teenager. When you add your teenager to your family's auto insurance policy, have him come with you to the insurance agent's office, so that he can be there while the agent explains not only his liability, but yours. Make sure the agent explains, as well, the liability that all of you can be exposed to if he drinks and drives, if he lets a friend drive, if he picks up a hitchhiker. He has to know the repercussions of unsafe or irresponsible driving.

Teenagers are going to be exposed to the temptations of drugs and underage drinking. It isn't enough that your teenager understand the personal health dangers of these things. She has to understand the legal repercussions, not only of doing them herself, but of being in the company of people who are committing illegal acts. Have a conference with your teenager and your family lawyer in which these liabilities are spelled out. He has to know *all* the ramifications of criminal behavior.

The more conferences with third-party authorities you can set up, the better. It includes your teenager in the process, which makes him feel he's being treated like an adult. And remember, you're still in that phase of evolution where it's assumed that you don't know anything.

There's a theme here, and it may be obvious, but I'm going to repeat it again anyway: Make sure your teenager understands *all* the ramifications of irresponsible behavior. Make sure he understands that "I didn't know" is no defense in a civil court or in a criminal court.

Roommates

One situation that can begin innocently and quickly spiral into problems of nightmare proportions is the roommate situation.

These nightmares happen all the time. A student came up to me after a recent college appearance and told me of his first experience sharing a house with two close friends. He had signed for the utilities in his name, and at the end of the semester, when they were way behind on the bill, his roommates skipped out without paying.

The friendship was shot, but so was his credit rating. He informed the utility company that his friends had run out on him, but that he would gladly pay his third of the bill.

Sorry, Charlie, they told him. Your name's on the account, you're responsible for the whole thing.

"I had no idea," he told me.

Well, he should have. But college is your teenager's first experience of total immersion in the outside world, and it's important to make sure she does know these things. She won't be coming home to your house at night anymore, and she won't be making her principal value transactions with people whose values she can predict.

Here's a worksheet she can use for setting up a household with roommates.

Roommate Responsibility Chart I:
Onetime Expenses or Responsibilities

Item	Dana	Kim	Chris
Lease: Who signs?			
Security Deposit			
Phone: In whose name?			
Deposit			
Utilities: In whose name?			
Deposit			
Cable TV: In whose name?			
Furniture and Appliances			
(by item)			

These are the onetime events—for each box, either check (whose name is it in?) or fill in a dollar amount (contribution to the deposit). For articles of furniture and appliances contributed to the apartment, write a name and dollar amount for each one. Keep this in a safe drawer or on somebody's (or everybody's) computer. Remember that whoever's name is on the lease, or the telephone, or the utilities, is legally responsible for it.

A second chart—and this one can go on the refrigerator, like the chore chart back at home—should be for regular expenses or responsibilities.

Further questions roommates should agree on in advance are:

- *overnight guests*. How many are allowed? How much advance notice has to be given? Who pays for their food?
- *pets* (if the lease allows for them).
- *noise and quiet times*.

Roommate Responsibility Chart II:
Regular Expenses or Responsibilities

Item	Dana		Kim		Chris	
	Do	Done	Do	Done	Do	Done
Pay rent						
Pay utility bill						
Pay phone bill						
Deal with repairs*						
Grocery shopping†						
Pay cable bill						
Clean kitchen						
Clean bathroom						
Clean living room						
Take out garbage						
Seasonal outdoor work						

Eighteen Years Old

When a teenager turns eighteen, his legal rights and obligations change. He is considered an adult in the eyes of the law. He may think he's the same person, but in crucial ways he is a totally different person, with new obligations and responsibilities, and you must make sure that he knows them.

He must register for the draft (if he's a male).

He's eligible to register and vote.

---

*Regular maintenance repairs, like a VCR that needs cleaning. Breakage should be handled by the person responsible.

†For jointly used staples (agreed upon in advance) like coffee. Unless the roommates all eat communally, individual food is bought and prepared individually.

A good way to use this is to check the "Do" box for whoever is assigned that task and the "Done" box when the task is completed. If it's a task that involves paying (like the rent or communal groceries or repairs), everyone checks the "Do" box, and the roommate who's assigned to do the actual bill paying for that month double-checks her "Do" box. She then must figure out the amount everyone owes, collect it (she checks off the others' "Done" boxes at this point), and pay the bill (now she checks off her own "Done" box).

He is considered, in many instances, old enough to sign legally binding contracts (the specifics vary here from state to state; an attorney should be consulted before your teenager enters into any legal situation).

You've always told your teenager that he has the power to say no to things that are not okay—now make sure he knows that now it's more important than ever to exercise that power.

Epilogue: Out the Door

Your baby . . . your toddler . . . your preschooler . . . your teenager . . . is grown-up. Leaving home. And he/she may be ready, but you're not.

What about all the advice you haven't given? Or the advice you think you gave, but you're not sure they got? What do you still absolutely have to, positively need to do?

A kiss would be a good idea.

Trust yourself . . . you've done all the rest. . . .

Trust your child . . . your new adult.

Index

alcohol, 179, 228
allowance, *see* jar system; work-for-pay
Angel Food East, 141
attention spans, 60
automobiles, 188

banking, *see* family banking
Bell, Don, 223–26
billboard game, 123–26
bingo money, 39–40
birthday gifts, *see* gifts
Black, Tyler, 61
Boston, Mass., Franklin's gift to, 24–25
breakage, monetary responsibility for, 60, 152–55, 171
Brokaw, Meredith, 144
Bronx Zoo, 173, 174
budgets:
    definition of, 21
    fixed vs. variable expenses and, 21–23
    gifts and, 76
    goal setting and, 24, 28
    for smart consumers, 161–63
    for teenagers, 201–6, 207–13

calculators, 49
career development, 166–69
    children's knowledge of parents' jobs and, 168–69
    entrepreneurship and, 167–68
    game for, 166–67

Carnegie Task Force for Early Child Care, 58
Center for Entrepreneurship, 168
change jars, 75
change-making game, 42–43, 49
charity, 13, 142, 144
    as family meeting topic, 83–84, 150–51
    goal setting for, 29
    in jar system, 74, 141, 146
    preschoolers and, 65–66
    teenagers and, 208
Chase Manhattan Bank, 12, 184
checkbooks, 72
child labor laws, 115
children, *see* preschoolers; school-agers; teenagers
Children's Financial Network, 12, 168
chores:
    Citizen of the Household, 52–53, 77, 110–12
    labor-management relations and, 117–21
    three categories of, 110–11
    "three strikes and you're out" rule for, 108
    see also odd jobs; work-for-pay
Christian, Spencer, 208
Christmas club, 76
Christmas detective game, 137–138
Citizen of the Community, 148–56
    breakage and, 152–55
    ethics and, 148–50

Citizen of the Community (*cont.*)
family meetings and, 150–52
shoplifting and, 155–56
value judgments and, 150
Citizen of the Household, 62, 73
chart for, 57, 110
chores, 52–53, 77, 110–12
obligations of, 114
and responsibility for others, 61
teenagers and, 185–89
clothing, 219–21
coin identification game, 39
college, time off before, 226–27
college funds, 56, 116, 144, 208
computers, 76, 117–18
conflict management, 222–23
Consumer Reports, 157
Consumer Resource Handbook, The,
151
consumers, *see* shopping; smart consumers
contracts, 129–35
for borrowing and lending money,
129–33
for odd jobs, 113, 114, 119–21
for trading, 134–35
verbal, 133–34
cooling-off periods, 126–27
corporate downsizing, 14–15
Cost Accounting (Horngren), 24*n*
counting, stacking, and change-making games, 40–44, 55
credit cards:
preschoolers' view of, 37
school–agers' understanding of, 72
secured, 96
teenagers and, 198–200
credit policy, in family banking,
96–100
curfews, 88, 187

Dacyczyn, Amy, 92
deferred gratification, 25, 56, 73, 75
games for, 44

"dissing," respect vs., 148
divorce, 186
different money rules and, 31–32
money as contributing factor in, 17,
31
divorce rate, family changes and, 14
"does it matter profoundly?," 187,
219
"don't pay too much, and don't pay too
little," 119
downsizing, corporate, 14–15
draws, 101
drugs, 126, 132, 179, 228
dusting, 107
Dworkin, Rabbi, 187, 219

education:
as attitude and process, 166
cost of, 15
as fixed expense, 22
job availability and, 15
saving for, 56, 116, 144, 208
Educational Resources, 76
entrepreneurship, 115–16, 166–68,
190–94
ethics, 148–50
expenses, fixed vs. variable, 21–23

family banking, 92–102
credit and, 96–100
investment and, 100–101
worksheets for, 92, 93–94
family finances:
as family meeting topic, 84–88
survey on attitudes toward, 19–20
family fund, 74, 92
family meetings, 77–91, 119, 136, 186
community issues and, 150–152
democracy and, 77, 102
format of, 78–79
importance of, 77–78
topics for, 81–91
FAO Schwarz, 12, 118
finding games, 46–47

First Children's Bank, 12, 118
First Women's Bank, 12, 169, 181–82
fixed expenses, 21–23
Forbes, 151
Franklin, Benjamin, 24–25
Freud, Sigmund, 32

Galápagos Islands, 172–73, 174
games:
    career development, 166–67
    Christmas detective, 137–38
    about ethics, 148–50
    need vs. want, 49–50, 122–26
    preschoolers' money games, 38–44,
        55
    preschoolers' shopping games,
        46–50
    smart consumer, 79
    teenagers' shopping games, 212–
        213
generational differences, 14–16, 171
"get it/spend it/save it/give it," 51
gift chits, 138–39
gifts, 136–47
    budgeting for, 76
    as family meeting topic, 83
    from grandparents, 32–33, 145–147
    guidelines for, 136–41, 143–44,
        145
    meaning of, 66
    receiving of, 142–43
Gilbar, Annie, 144
goal setting, 24, 26–30
    for budgets, 24, 28
    for charity, 29
    for earning income, 27
    for household sharing, 28–29
    for saving, 27–28
    for spending, 28
Golden Rule, 18
Good Citizen Chart, 57
grandparents, gifts from, 32–33,
    145–47
Gresham's law, 16

holidays and holiday gifts, *see* gifts
homework, 113
honesty, 67, 172–73
Horngren, Charles, 24n
household rules, *see* rules

income, goal setting for, 27
interest, 23, 72
    on children's savings, 74–75
    on family bank loans, 98–99
investing, 100–101, 214–18

Jamaica, 101
jar system, 72, 141
    cash gifts and, 146
    expansion of, 73–76
    three jars, 55–56
    see also penalty jars; quick change
        jar
job charts:
    for preschoolers, 54–55
    for school-agers, 104–7
jobs, for children, *see* career
        development; chores;
        entrepreneurship
job stability, 14–15
Junior Achievement, 168

Kids as Customers (McNeal), 71n
kitchen games, 43–44
kitty litter, changing of, 105–6, 108–
    109

labor force, women in, 14, 183–84
laundry, 107
lawn service, 120–21
lions, acquisition of, 173–74
listening, art of, 78
littering, as "dissing," 148
long-term goals, 24
long-term savings jar, 56, 75, 146

McNeal, James U., 71
major purchase decisions, 81–83

Make-a-Wish Foundation, 151
medium-term savings jar, 55–56, 73,
    75, 101, 126, 146, 208
Miner, Sydny, 134
money:
    borrowing and lending of, 96–100,
        129–33, 135
    divorce and, 17, 31
    Gresham's law and, 16
    importance of learning about,
        16–18, 30
    preschoolers' games for, 38–44,
        55
    preschoolers' understanding of,
        37–38
    as social tool, 12–13
    teenagers' education about, 181–85,
        190–94
    time value of, 24–25
money bingo, 39–40
Money Doesn't Grow on Trees (God-
    frey), 12, 172–73
Mr. Potato Head, 166–67
music, career in, 223–26
mutual funds, 100, 216, 218

National Council on Economic Educa-
    tion, 168
National Wildlife Fund, 144
needs:
    game for, 49–50, 122–26
    of infants, 58
    nutrition and, 160
    as parental responsibility, 51,
        128
    wants vs., 22, 91, 122–28, 162
New York State Lottery, 181
New York Times, 15n, 183n
New York Times Book Review,
    173
Nolan, Jennifer Rockefeller, 64
"not okay" behavior, 188
"no work, no pay," 107–8
nutrition, 160

obligations, three kinds of, 113–14
odd jobs, 110, 111
    contracts and pay for, 113, 114,
        119–21
    list of, 112–13
    soliciting of, 114–15
One to One, 168
Oprah Winfrey Show, The, 11–12, 16,
    30, 48, 108, 140–41, 143
Opus 40, 141

paperweights, rocks as, 115–16
parents:
    children's knowledge of work of,
        168–69
    messages to children from, 170–
        174
    responsibilities of, 51, 128
parties, 188
partnerships, for investing, 101
"paycheck shock," 74
penalty jars, 92–95
Penny Whistle Party Planner and
    Birthday Party Book, The
    (Brokaw and Gilbar), 144
personal obligations, 113
Podmayerski, John, 120
potty training, 58
preschoolers, 35–68
    attention spans of, 60
    developmental differences in, 49
    in family meetings, 78
    money as viewed by, 37–38
    money games for, 38–44, 55
    shopping games for, 46–50
    taxes explained to, 48–49
    three jar system for, 55–56
    values and, 58–68
    work-for-pay for, 50–57
price tag games, 41–42
PRODIGY Service, 19
product test reports, 79–81
"proud charts," 109
punishment:

fairness of, 61, 171
for not doing something, 59, 109, 171
for shoplifting, 155
see also penalty jar
purchasing power, 24

quick change jar, 55, 60, 75, 80, 126,
    146, 208
Quicken, 117

Ravich, George, 19
reinforcement:
    of values, 59, 63
    verbal, 54, 57
replacement, of consumable items,
    188
responsibility, 25, 55
    parental, 51, 128
    preschoolers and, 61-63, 67
    roommates and, 229-31
    teenagers' legal, 231-32
restaurant bills, 72
"Ringo for President," as sidewalk slo-
    gan, 152-53
rites of passage, 110, 180
rock painting, 115
Ronald McDonald House, 151
roommates, 229-31
rules:
    "does it matter profoundly?," 187,
        219
    "don't pay too much, and don't pay
        too little," 119
    as family meeting topic, 88-91
    negotiable vs. nonnegotiable, 22,
        187
    "no work, no pay," 107-8
    for quick cash purchases, 55, 126
    for teenagers, 187-89
    "three strikes and you're out," 108
    for work-for-pay, 104-9

Sales, Soupy, 44
Salvation Army, 168

Saturday Box, 61-62
savings:
    goal setting for, 27-28
    long-term, 56
    medium-term, 55-56
    rates of, 71
    strategies for, 100
school-agers, 69-174
    career development and, 166-69
    Citizen of the Household chores and
        odd jobs and, 110-16
    as Citizens of the Community,
        148-56
    contracts and, 129-35
    determining financial skills of, 72
    developmental levels of, 85, 103
    discretionary spending by, 71
    expanded jar system for, 73-76
    family banking and, 92-102
    family meetings and, 77-91
    gifts and, 136-47
    labor-management relations be-
        tween parents and, 117-21
    needs of, wants vs., 122-28
    parents' messages to, 170-74
    secured credit cards for, 96
    smart consumer tips for, 157-
        165
    work-for-pay for, 103-9
secured credit cards, 96
self-esteem, 16, 17-18, 135, 155
sentimental value, 67-68
sewer tours, scaring children on,
    115
Shakespeare, William, 129, 155
sharing:
    goal setting and, 28-29
    preschoolers and, 63-65
shoplifting, 155-56
shopping, 45
    games for, 46-50
    see also smart consumers
short-term goals, 24
smart consumer game, 79

smart consumers, 157–65
  budgets for, 161–63
  checklist for, 157
  nutrition and, 160
  time value of money and, 160–61
  time value of time and, 163–165
  world as classroom for, 158–159
stock market, 214–18
success, 221–22
Sunshine for HIV Kids, 141, 151
su-su, 101

taxes, 170
  in jar system, 73–74, 146
  preschoolers' first exposure to, 48–49
  teenagers and, 208
teenagers, 175–232
  budgets for, 201–6, 207–13
  as Citizens of the Household, 185–89
  and consequences of actions, 228–32
  credit cards and, 198–200
  discretionary spending by, 181
  entrepreneurship and, 190–94
  financial responsibility of, 207–13
  investing by, 214–18
  legal responsibilities of, 231–32
  money education and skills for, 181–85, 190–94
  and preparation for leaving home, 195–200
  real life lessons for, 181–89, 208–12, 219–27
  rules for, 187–89
  transition years for, 177–80
telephone message-taking, 89–90
television commercials, 81, 158–59

thank-you notes, 143
three jars, *see* jar system
"three strikes and you're out," 108
Tightwad Gazette, The (Dacyczyn), 92
"time out," 59
time value:
  of money, 24–25, 160–61
  of time, 25, 59, 163–65, 171
tipping, 72, 73
toys, Saturday Box for, 61–62
Toys for Tots, 66
trading, 134–35

UNICEF, 12, 13, 66, 84, 141, 144, 151

vacation funds, 100
vacation planning, 83
value judgments, 150
values:
  ethics, 148–50
  preschoolers and, 58–68
variable expenses, 21–23
verbal contracts, 133–34
verbal reinforcement, 54, 57
volunteer work, 141

Walker, Susan, 38, 134
wants, needs vs., 22, 91, 122–28, 162
what's it worth?, 41
Willard, Nancy, 68
women, in labor force, 14, 183–84
Word for Windows, 184
work-for-pay, 77, 114, 155, 190
  job charts for, 54–55
  pay rates and, 53, 110
  for preschoolers, 50–57
  rules for, 54
  for school-agers, 103–9